SYRACUSE UNIVERSITY
An Architectural Guide

SYRACUSE
An Architectural Guide
UNIVERSITY

JEFFREY GORNEY

SYRACUSE UNIVERSITY PRESS

Library of Congress Cataloging-in-Publication Data
Gorney, Jeffrey.
Syracuse University : an architectural guide / Jeffrey Gorney.—1st ed.
p.   cm.
Includes bibliographical references.
ISBN 0-8156-0810-1 (pbk. : alk. paper)
1. Syracuse University—Buildings—Guidebooks.
2. Syracuse (N.Y.)—Buildings, structures, etc.—Guidebooks.
I. Title.

LD5234.G67 2006
378.747'66—dc22   2006012173

JEFFREY GORNEY is a writer and photographer in Syracuse. His arti-
cles and photos on historic preservation have appeared in the *Syracuse
Post-Standard, Renewing Syracuse, FOCUS Greater Syracuse,* and in
materials for downtown Syracuse and neighborhood associations.

CONTENTS

DONORS

Supported in part with a grant from
The Greenwald Haupt Vision Fund,
Harry R. Greenwald, director.

Syracuse University Departments
    Design and Construction, Eric Beattie
    Housing, Meal Plan, & ID Services, David Kohr
    Purchasing, Allan C. Breese

FOREWORD

ERIC BEATTIE, OFFICE OF DESIGN AND CONSTRUCTION

Syracuse University: An Architectural Guide is not only fascinating reading but also the ideal companion for a sidewalk tour of this illustrious campus. My hope is that those who are unfamiliar with the delights of SU's buildings and gardens will take it along with them as they explore. Strolling through the Old Row one can easily imagine what collegiate life in the late nineteenth and early twentieth centuries must have been like. Fortunately, much of the fundamental pedagogic framework of college life from those early days—lectures, studios, labs, and studying—remains essential to university life today, a fact demonstrated by the highly effective functioning for today's academic endeavors of early buildings such as the Hall of Languages (1871–73), Crouse College (1887–89), and Tolley Hall (1888–89). It is with great pride that we preserve these landmark buildings as testimonies to the University's past while carefully adapting them to meet the needs of the University's future.

The campus building booms of the 1920s and the era following World War II, like the current boom in building as we enter the twenty-first century, challenged campus planners to create stimulating and effective expansions of the campus, not only to meet the immediate needs of a thriving and growing University but to leave flexible opportunities for the campus to adapt to the inevitable next set of academic challenges. The result is an eclectic composition of architectural styles and forms, creating a rich environment in which to learn and live. The broad architectural range of the campus both expresses and stimulates the diverse interests and objectives of the University, and the result is an environment that encourages students to appreciate and learn from the past while preparing for a future that will continue to evolve and provide new challenges.

Working your way from the northern edge of the main campus along University Avenue across the front lawn and the quad to the top of Mount Olympus can give you an appreciation for the scale of the campus and its buildings. But once you stand atop Mount Olympus, be prepared to take in its loftier view of the campus, from the residence halls at the edge of Thornden Park extending west all the way to the Center of Excellence and the Warehouse in the heart of downtown Syracuse. Look also to the south, from the Lampe Athletic Complex to the long slope of South Campus, with its many and varied facilities. The Syracuse University Campus is an expansive, fully functional academic village with its arms open wide to the world.

Recent and soon-to-be-completed buildings, such as the School of Management, Newhouse III, the Center of Excellence, and the Life Sciences facility, help define an era of modern architecture that maintains Syracuse's tradition of building in the style of the times. I fully expect that one hundred years from now a new guide to our campus will proudly point to these carefully preserved buildings that helped shape a successful twenty-first century for the University.

ACKNOWLEDGMENTS

First and foremost, I want to gratefully acknowledge Virginia Denton, whose fine work vastly informs this book. Next, I thank Christopher Danek, whose careful reading of the manuscript contributed significantly to its final form. I am further indebted to John Robert Greene, for his books on the history of Syracuse University, and to Evamaria Hardin, for her book, *Syracuse Landmarks*, which proved to be an invaluable resource.

Also, I want to thank the Syracuse University Archives, Syracuse University Photo and Imaging Center, Syracuse University Office of Special Events, Syracuse Office of News and Publications, *Syracuse Record*, and Syracuse University Department of Athletic Communications for the use of images from their collections. These images are the property of Syracuse University and are collectively credited to the University in the book. Unless otherwise noted, the photographs are courtesy of the author.

SYRACUSE UNIVERSITY

An Architectural Guide

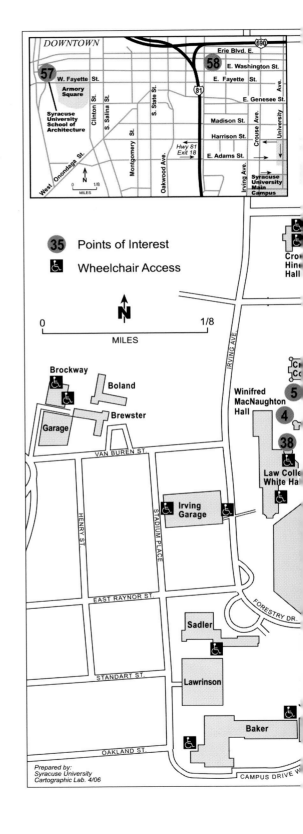

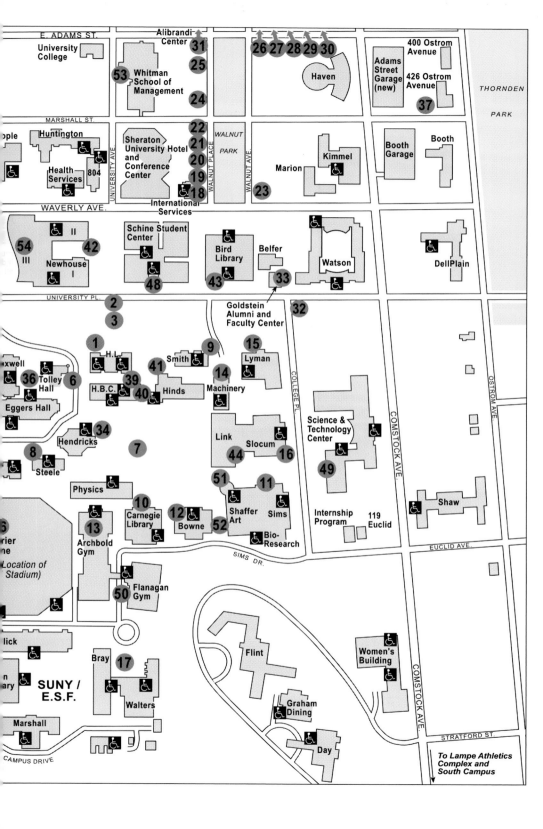

THE HILL

The University shall . . . demonstrate the perfect har-
mony and indissoluble oneness of all that is valuable of the
old and new

—Reverend Jesse Peck[1]

In August 1871 Syracuse University held its first inaugural ceremonies. At its conclusion Bishop Jesse Peck laid the cornerstone of the Hall of Languages. Known for his way with words, Peck dedicated the University to the "diffusion of knowledge . . . and the promotion of . . . learning, literature, and science."[2]

Much has changed since then, yet the school's mission remains the same: the pursuit of excellence. This guide provides a narrative and architectural tour of the Syracuse University campus, showing how it evolved to reflect and support the culture and character of academic community and urban environs. Intended for prospective students, alumni, faculty, and visitors, this guide offers an inside look at the University's most engaging structures set against significant moments in its history. Here are the chancellors and architects, the benefactors and builders whose vision and grit gave the campus shape and substance. Here too are the grand triumphs and false starts, external events and internal choices that transformed a small bucolic school into a culturally complex multiversity. Here is the once and future architectural heritage of Syracuse University.

Ask anyone who comes to the University and they will tell you of a campus set high on a splendid hill. On a clear day those who study, work, or visit here can look out from the Hill onto a panoramic view of city, countryside, and Onondaga Lake.

Had it been up to Andrew Dickson White, things might have taken a different turn. White was a prominent citizen of nineteenth-century Syracuse who happened also to be the president of Cornell. He wanted *his* university to reside on the Hill and took the matter right to founder Ezra Cornell. But Ezra, who had other ideas, built Cornell on his own farmland, along the shores of Cayuga Lake, and Syracuse University came to make its home on the Hill.

Over the years the campus at SU grew into a mélange of architectural styles that has elicited both controversy and praise. More than a commitment to eclecticism, the evolution of this campus suggests a carefully considered response to change. This University shaped itself around economic booms and busts, cycles of urban indifference and sensitivity, reckless demolition and inventive building—and the pursuit of merit.

As suggested by Reverend Peck, early administrators found that the key to successful planning lay in the past, that yesterday's patterns can show where buildings should and should not be placed and how to better mold a campus green. To fully appreciate the SU campus today one must explore its roots.

ROOTS

Syracuse University had its origins in the Genesee Wesleyan Seminary. Founded in 1832 by the Genesee Methodist Conference, the seminary was situated in Lima, New York, south of Rochester. Seven years earlier the new Erie Canal had transformed central New York. Linking industrial downstate cities with fertile farmland upstate—and the Midwest—the Canal spurred cultural, economic, and educational invention. Religious movements such as Methodism began to flourish, prompting the creation of new institutions.

The circuit-riding ministers who started the Genesee Seminary chose Lima because the town offered the most money for the new school. There, in

Genesee Wesleyan Seminary, 1842. Courtesy of Syracuse University Archives

recent wilderness, they constructed an academy building in Greek Revival style. The new institution they chartered was committed to educating "persons of any race or color, whether male or female."³ Its inaugural student body consisted of four men and one woman.

But like other new nineteenth-century institutions, Genesee had pursued ambitions beyond its resources. New technology and a remote location further compounded its difficulties; railroads had replaced the Erie Canal as an economic catalyst, yet no train stopped at far-off Lima. Furthermore, in 1849 the Seminary created a companion institution called Genesee College. Still its fortunes did not improve. In 1866, after years of struggle, the trustees of Genesee College decided to seek a locale that offered better economic and transportation benefits.

Ninety miles to the east, the bustling Erie Canal port of Syracuse had embarked upon a search of its own. The new rail age had expanded canal prosperity, turning Syracuse into a boomtown. Her citizens yearned for something

Genesee College, 1866. Courtesy of Syracuse University Archives

more, something not yet identified. "What gives to Oxford and Cambridge, England, to Edinburgh, Scotland, to New Haven, Connecticut, their most lustrous names abroad?" observed a local writer. "Their Universities. Syracuse has all the advantages: business, social, and religious—let her add the educational and she adds to her reputation, her desirability."[4]

Galvanized for action, the port of Syracuse set out to become the new home to Genesee College in the face of aggressive competition from other communities like Rome, New York. Syracuse, however, raised extensive funds and mounted an ambitious and successful campaign. In 1869, after a year of dispute, a convention of Methodist ministers chose Syracuse over the others. Lima raised a fuss about the "removal" as they called it.[5] Lawsuits and angry words flew back and forth. But soon the deal was sealed. In 1870 an incorporation certificate for the new university was filed in Albany, the State Board of Regents granted the school a charter, and Syracuse University replaced Genesee College.

That same year, board trustee and prominent local banker George F. Comstock offered the school fifty acres of hilly farmland on a hillside southeast of the city center, part of the negotiation that brought it to Syracuse.

Meanwhile, the seminary move to Syracuse ignited unexpected controversy. Among the forty-one members of the first Class of 1871 were several students from Genesee. Would the new Syracuse University, they wondered, sustain progressive "co-ed" policies initiated by the old Genesee? First chairman of the board Reverend Peck insisted that admissions be open to all qualified persons, regardless of sex. First chancellor Reverend Haven agreed.

Male students objected loudly, and an article in the campus paper stated, "women's inability to learn was an established fact." None of which discouraged seven spirited young ladies from enrolling in the first class, among them Reverend Haven's bright daughter, Frances.

Reverend Peck also contributed $50,000 for the new school's endowment, gleaned from moneys he had earned in lecture fees. Nonetheless, it was a difficult birth, there was squabbling amid the church founders, and Comstock's land was contested before acceptance.

In January 1871, Reverend Peck drafted "a general outline of the plan of buildings" for the university. Peck described what was, in effect, the University's earliest master plan. His design kindled excitement. Seven new buildings were to be constructed on Comstock's hillside. Each building was to be dedicated to a different academic discipline.

As is often the case with grand plans, little of it came to be at first. Yet in selecting a site and seeding it with buildings, SU founders exerted a weighty influence upon the future campus. Both the act itself and subsequent development allowed SU to serve as an archetype of the American university campus.

Peck's was a vision of stylistic eclecticism. On one occasion he declared that the new university should "demonstrate the perfect harmony and indissoluble oneness of all that is valuable in the old and the new."[6] It was an inventive approach at the time, and it would steer university planners for years to come.

Like so many other American colleges of the nineteenth century, the University was housed in a single broad and tall building at the urban perimeter—in this instant, on a hilltop farm looking down on the town as if from a fortress. On August 31, 1871, the foundation stone was laid for the first building on campus, the Hall of Languages.

1. *Hall of Languages, 1871–73*

Cost: $136,000

Architect: Horatio Nelson White, Syracuse

Remodeling of interior: 1979; Builders: Sargent Webster
Crenshaw & Folley, Syracuse; Design consultants: Architectural
Resources Cambridge, Cambridge, Mass.

During construction of the Hall of Languages, University classes were held in downtown Syracuse at a rented commercial site on East Genesee and Montgomery Streets, named the Myers Block.

Upon completion of the building in 1873, students and faculty assembled downtown for the last time to march in proud parade to their new home on "piety hill." The subject of the first lecture to be given on the new campus was, appropriately, "Gothic Architecture."

Hall of Languages. Courtesy of Syracuse University Archives

Myers Block. Courtesy of Syracuse University Archives

Built during the term of SU's first chancellor, Alexander Winchell, the Hall of Languages remains perhaps the most compelling structure on campus. It may be hard to believe but in 1873 the hill upon which this landmark building stands was a hayfield. Rain turned the ground to mud, soiling the hems of long skirts and caking leather boots with sludge. Before its grand stairway was constructed, the Hall of Languages was fronted by wooden boardwalks that clattered with the sound of freshmen and sophomores playing games of tug-of-war. Grass grew high. Cows grazed on "campus." A $200 profit from the sale of hay paid for the mortgage but not, it seems, the architect's fee.

University trustees considered several prominent architects including W. L. Woollett of Albany and Archimedes Russell. Eventually they chose the celebrated Horatio White of Syracuse. White designed a graceful H-shaped structure of Onondaga limestone in the then-popular Second Empire style. Floors throughout were wood; twin rooftop towers held water tanks in case of fire, and a vast chapel occupied the entire second floor. Two elegant side doors opened onto the caretaker's apartment and the boiler room. A center cupola clock was added to the building front in 1887.

Hall of Languages cupola with clock. Courtesy of Syracuse University Archives

Elegance notwithstanding, within fifty years of construction the building interior had begun to deteriorate. Such early decline indicated that the original builders placed significant effort and resources on exterior masonry, a fairly typical scenario for nineteenth-century academic structures.

Beginning in 1977, the Hall of Languages was renovated, yet its imposing exterior was kept intact. At that time a fifth floor was incorporated into the interior. This alteration was not driven by the need for more space. Rather its intent was to create a diaphragm for lateral support of the exterior masonry shell as each of the original floors was removed, top to bottom. An interior scissor stairs recedes while rising to compensate visually for lost ceiling height.

Refurbishment was complete within fourteen months. During that time occupants used the upper section of the Archbold Gymnasium (currently the gymnastics area). Restoration of the Hall of Languages, upon its completion, earned an Honor Award from the American Institute of Architects.

From the outset, this first building housed the College of Liberal Arts. Today it provides classroom space for over two thousand students and offices for several departments, including English and textual studies, philosophy, and religion.

2. *Gateway to Campus*

The intersection of University Avenue and University Place has traditionally been regarded as the entrance to campus, although buildings now extend beyond it in several directions. The current divided stairway of limestone and granite is relatively new, yet the walkway leading to the Hall of Languages remains an enduring singular reminder of the early campus. The original staircase was a gift of the Class of 1914.

Gateway, with divided stairway

3. *A Place of Remembrance, 1990*

The entrance to the University from University Place is axially aligned with the entrance to the Hall of Languages. At the esplanade one sees the Place of Remembrance: a simple, elegant tribute to the thirty-five SU students who perished in the Pan Am Flight 103 crash over Lockerbie, Scotland, December 21, 1988. Often it is bedecked with memorial flowers, cards, and mementos from family and friends of the deceased.

Place of Remembrance

THE EARLY YEARS

While the Hall of Languages was going up on his old property, George Comstock purchased two-hundred acres of the Stevens farm to the north of University Place. Here, in 1872, he established Walnut Park, centerpiece of his new "Highlands" subdivision. Comstock deeded the park to the city with the proviso that it be landscaped, planted, and maintained in a manner befitting a fine public commons.

Comstock was not alone. Even at its beginnings university evolution was closely tied to that of the city and, particularly, the neighborhood in which it was placed. Many early university trustees were wealthy business leaders who combined active philanthropy with economic self-interest. Real estate development figured largely among their concerns.

To counter expansion by the University and to maintain the Highlands as an exclusive area, Comstock successfully sold residential plots to the local elite. In due time a lush greensward extended north from University Place, framed on either side by large and gracious homes.

From the start Comstock wanted Syracuse University and the Highlands to develop as an integrated upscale entity. A contemporary account describes the latter as "a beautiful town . . . springing up on the hillside and a community of refined and cultivated membership . . . established near the spot which will soon be the center of a great and beneficent educational institution." [7]

Still incensed over loss of the Genesee Seminary, residents of Lima predicted failure for the new Syracuse University. Horatio White had in fact been commissioned to design six buildings stylistically similar to the Hall of Languages, including the Halls of Science, Philosophy, and History. But when a major bank failure precipitated the Panic of 1873, the ensuing economic depression nearly toppled the University, bringing all campus construction to a halt. For the next fourteen years the Hall of Languages would house the entire school, lone evidence of the University's First Campus Plan and a constant reminder of grand ambition thwarted and the power of external events.

By the time Charles N. Sims became third chancellor in 1881, the Hill had become known as the Hill of Knowledge. Be that as it may, the school was now mired in perilous debt, to the tune of $173,000. "You cannot save the university," said outgoing chancellor Erastus O. Haven to Sims, "it must go."[8] But Haven did not know with whom he was dealing. By the late 1800s Sims had, through "patient labors and financial sacrifices," salvaged the school from indebtedness.

With its financial future seemingly on terra firma, the University pursued a new era of physical expansion. Construction, by the end of the 1880s, had resumed on the south side of University Place. New buildings did not follow Peck's original plan but went up one by one as funds or donors appeared. Holden Observatory was built in 1887, followed by two Romanesque Revival buildings, von Ranke Library (1889) and Crouse College (1889).

Tuition fees in the 1890s amounted to $60 per year in liberal arts and $100 in fine arts and medicine. An advertisement of the day trumpeted SU as having "four colleges . . . elegant buildings . . . seventy professors . . . 900 students." Courses led to the A.B. degree with Latin, Greek, English, mathematics, and gym required during the first two years. Members of the Glee and Mandolin Club performed once a year in Crouse Auditorium.

Yet for all its newfound status, the campus was not quite a polished affair. There were no dormitories, although freshmen could rent a room in the area for $3.00 per month. Dwellings were chilly and lit by kerosene. There was no athletic field. There were no driveways. Chancellor Sims pastured his cow on campus.

4. *Holden Observatory, 1887*

Architect: Archimedes Russell, Syracuse
Moved: 1991; Movers: L. D. Dexheimer & Son, Guilford, N.Y.

This second building on campus was funded and furnished by local coal merchant and SU Trustee Erastus F. Holden. Astronomy had been in vogue since the University's beginnings, and this observatory was dedicated as a memorial to Holden's son, Charles Demarest Holden, an earlier graduate of SU.

One of the best remembered moments at Holden Observatory occurred in 1939 when Mars passed close to Earth. An eager public waited in long lines until 3 A.M. to view the red planet.

Holden Observatory. Courtesy of Syracuse University Archives

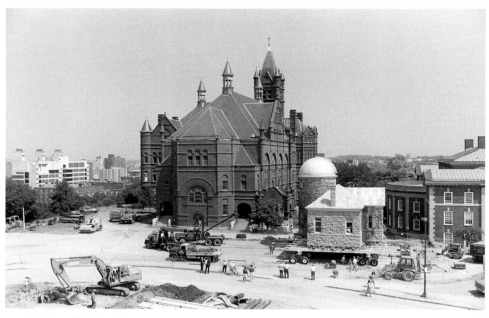

Moving Holden Observatory, 1991. Courtesy of Syracuse University Archives

Hailed by local papers as an "observatory of the first magnitude," the building seemed as mysterious as the heavens with its paved exterior of Onondaga limestone, blackened mortar, and lead-coated copper roof. All have since been restored. Three-foot-thick walls shielded a telescope with an electric clock drive, three-inch reversible transit, chronograph, and a chronometer. Built by Alvin Clark and Sons of Cambridge, Mass., then the world's foremost telescope company, the futuristic instrument was mounted on a "pier of masonry" to prevent vibrations. The "telescope room," as it was called, comprised a thirty-foot tower crowned by a rotating dome. To keep its viewing slot aligned with the scope, the dome is set on rollers and rotated manually. The SU Department of Physics still uses the scope for purposes of instruction.

At the opening of the observatory, Dr. Simon Newcomb of Washington, D.C., gave a fitting talk on "The Place of Astronomy in the Sciences." The planet Pluto would not be discovered for another forty years, and general understanding of the stars and space was limited at best.

Chancellor Sims had positioned Holden Observatory on a small rise southwest of the Hall of Languages, "to provide an unimpeded view of the heavens" for students and public alike to enjoy. That fine sightline vanished two years later when Crouse College was erected in front of the observatory.

A motion to move Holden from its home on "Science Hill" to Mt. Olympus was proposed soon after its construction, but the move never came to pass. On June 27, 1991, however, the observatory was relocated to make room for Eggers Hall, as part of the Maxwell School expansion. It took twelve girders and eighty wheels to maneuver the rock solid, 320-ton structure to a site 190 feet to the southwest and 60 feet to the south. Because Holden was a national landmark, workers took great pains to ensure its safekeeping. Proceeding at a rate of four inches per hour, the move was an exacting effort that took three days. To underscore confidence, the relocation contractor placed a full glass of water on a table within the observatory during each day of the move. None of it spilled!

5. *Crouse College, 1887–89*

Cost: $500,000
Architect: Archimedes Russell, Syracuse
Partial restoration: 1974; Architects: Office of Design and
    Construction, Syracuse University, Syracuse

Built for the growing School of Fine Arts, Crouse College was a gift of local merchant, SU trustee and banker John R. Crouse. Because he intended it to foster women's education, it was originally called the John Crouse College for Women, but it was coeducational from the start.

The Syracuse University College of Fine Arts was the first in the country to award a degree in the field of fine arts.

John Crouse wanted his building to be "the best in the country . . . no matter the cost." Crouse chose an impressive building site, high on the Hill, and was even allowed to oversee construction, only to die shortly before its completion. His son Edgar took over. For a half-million dollars, he fulfilled his father's vision.

The structure was made of Longmeadow sandstone on a granite base. Initially called "brownstone," it was quarried from an area southeast of Springfield, Massachusetts, part of the "red bed" basin of the Connecticut River valley and the Newark basin of New Jersey and Eastern Pennsylvania.

In its mass, pitched roofs and its detail and ornamentation, Crouse College epitomized Richardsonian Romanesque, a style popular in America from 1880 to 1900. It was named for British architect Henry Hobson Richardson but went out of fashion due to the high cost of stone facing techniques at the time.

Opening in September 1889, Crouse College was an exercise in Victorian excess that delighted the public but drew frost from the critics. Writer Mont-

Crouse College

gomery Schuyler criticized Russell's stylistic indulgence as a "random aggregation of unstudied form and features."[9] More recently journalist David Ramsey noted that Schuyler "had a point. Crouse College roars into the sky as a celebration of architectural anarchy."[10]

Crouse College stood in stark contrast to the Hall of Languages as a commitment to the contemporary of its time. To the north, where it overlooked the city, it served to form the Old Row, which is described on page 26. To the south, on the site of the current Quad, lay plowed fields.

Then again, the building was meant to display its founder's wealth and largess. A carved wood staircase leads to Memorial Music Hall on the fourth floor. Setnor Memorial Auditorium, as it is called today, seats up to 1,200. Leaded stained glass windows in the auditoriums and south stair were the fine work of Henry Keck, a local craftsman of national renown.

Architectural historian Evamaria Hardin observes, "With its open-timber ceiling and stained-glass windows [Setnor] is one of the finest interior spaces

Setnor Auditorium, Crouse College

at the University. You may want to sit here on an afternoon," she suggests, "when the stained-glass windows color the rays of the sun that model the room's surfaces and highlight its tactile qualities."

A terra-cotta bell tower, gift of the senior Crouse, remains a time-honored symbol of the University. To the delight of students and passersby, it still chimes several times a day. The chimes, also a gift of John D. Crouse, were always played by members of the Delta Kappa Epsilon fraternity except for a period during World War II when the sisters of Alpha Phi sorority took over the task.

During the early postwar era, much of the interior beaded ceiling wood-work in Crouse was painted purple and gray. From the late 1940s into the early 1950s, most corridor floors were covered with layers of resilient flooring, and new suspended overhead surfaces concealed many of the original studio ceilings. Under a long-range restoration plan begun in the mid-1970s, these alterations were removed. At that time an etched door was replaced and a transom glass replicated by a student in the School of Art.

6. *Tolley Hall,* 1888–89 *(former von Ranke Library)*

Cost: $34,000
Architect: Archimedes Russell, Syracuse
Addition of west wing: 1903; Architect: Frederick Revels, Syracuse

In the late 1880s, Reverend John M. Reid, president of Genesee College, presented the University with the collected books of Leopold von Ranke, a noted historian of the day. At least sixty-nine donors helped raise funds to cover construction costs for an appropriate library building. Reflecting its use as a repository for rare books, the structure was nearly fireproof. Made of russet brick on a granite base, its Victorianized Romanesque façade featured corner turrets and towers, terra-cotta detail, Queen Anne accents, and Richardsonian Romanesque mass. All of these features recalled Crouse College, built at the same time. A west wing, added in 1903, changed the basic building shape from asymmetrical to symmetrical. It was in the basement of von Ranke Library that the first cafeteria on campus was situated.

Tolley Hall is named after William P. Tolley who served as chancellor of Syracuse University from 1942 to 1969.

By 1907 the building book collection had outgrown its space and was transferred to Carnegie Library, making that the official main library at SU. Originally von Ranke's south end was a two-story reading room surrounded by stacks and balconies with access from the main north entrance. After the collection move, the reading room was floored over and a south door added. On September 14, 1985, von Ranke Library was christened anew as the Tolley Administration Building. Until 2005 the Tolley Administration Building served as the offices of the chancellor and vice chancellor. It is

Von Ranke Library. Courtesy of Syracuse University Archives

presently being renovated to house the Center for the Humanities and area studies programs.

Together with the Hall of Languages, these first buildings (Holden Observatory, Crouse College, and von Ranke Library) formed the basis for the Old Row. This grouping, along with its companion Lawn, established one of Syracuse's most enduring images. "Its emphatically linear organization along the brow of the hill follows a tradition of American campus planning which dates to the construction of the 'Yale Row' in the 1790s." [11] At SU, the Old Row continued to provide framework for growth well into the twentieth century.

The first exception to this linear pattern was the placement of the Women's Gymnasium (1891) in the hayfield behind the Hall of Languages. By turning its back on stylistic uniformity and embracing the Romanesque, the University set the template for architectural eclecticism.

The Women's Gymnasium (which later became the Journalism Building) was demolished in 1965, but at the time of its construction, the surrounding

Hall of Languages, von Ranke Library, and Crouse College, ca. 1889. Courtesy of Syracuse University Archives

Grading the Old Oval behind the Gymnasium and the Hall of Languages, ca. 1895. Courtesy of Syracuse University Archives

empty land was graded and turned into an athletic field and faculty vegetable garden. Loosely framed by buildings on two sides, the Old Oval, as students called the field, joined the Lawn in a new open campus space. Such modest beginnings did not hint at its eventual significance: the Old Oval would become the Main Quad.

7. *The Quad*

At the crossroads of the contemporary campus can be found the Main Quad. Considered the heart of college life at SU, its walkways are well-traveled paths between classes. In fair weather Quad benches and grasses stir with students at play or in thought or study.

In 1899, James Roscoe Day became fourth chancellor of Syracuse University. At six-foot-three and 230 pounds, with long sideburns and one glass eye, the former Methodist minister was a larger-than-life figure whose no-nonsense manner caused him to be called the "iron chancellor."

Under Day's tenure, growth of the physical campus would be extraordinary, especially in the spheres of engineering and the sciences.

The Quad. Courtesy of Syracuse University Archives

8. *Steele Hall, 1898*

Cost: $46,000
Architect: Edwin H. Gaggin, Syracuse University School of
    Architecture, Syracuse
Builders: Dickinson & Van Wagner

A severe yet modified Renaissance style distinguished the strong presence of Steele Hall, first science building at the University. Constructed seven years after the Women's Gymnasium, Steele Hall defined another open space on campus, west of the Gymnasium and south of Crouse College. Initially called the Esther Baker Steele Hall of Physics, it was built to provide much needed classroom space for the science department, which had been lodged in the Hall of Languages. Mrs. Steele, who contributed funds for the laboratory, was both friend and trustee of the University. Many of the University's administrative offices are currently located in Steele Hall, including the Office of Student Affairs and the Office of the Registrar.

Steele Hall

9. *Smith Hall,* 1902

Cost: $75,000

Architects: Gaggin & Gaggin, Syracuse

Lyman C. Smith, founder of L. C. Smith and Brothers Typewriter Company, wanted to start a college specializing in degrees for civil, electrical, and mechanical engineers. The idea was to supply toolmakers and mechanics for his business. The result was the Lyman C. Smith College of Applied Science, the University's first engineering school.

The L. C. Smith Typewriter Company became Smith-Corona Typewriter, a major player in the industrial heyday of Syracuse.

Smith Hall fronts University Place with a rough masonry face of Ohio sandstone enhanced by unexpected classical ornamentation. Two symmetrical towers with inset arched windows are topped by red tile. When the building opened, there were laboratories in the basement and machine shops on the first floor. A huge drafting room occupied the entire top story. Today this building houses the College of Visual and Performing Arts programs.

Smith Hall

THE EARLY
TWENTIETH CENTURY

The first decade of the twentieth century was a time of firsts for Syracuse University. On September 15, 1903, the *first* issue of the *Daily Orange* was published, the nation's *first* collegiate news to feature cartoons.

This period also saw construction of the *first* dormitories on campus, Haven Hall (1898) and Winchell Hall (1900). Both were named for prior chancellors. Both have since been torn down to make way for new buildings. While Smith Hall (1902) created for the College of Applied Sciences, reinforced the development of the old style, the new dormitories represented a different kind of planning concept.

The earliest campus was a single row of buildings fronting on University Place. Winchell and Haven Halls, placed on the north side of University Place, now served to bookend the University Avenue axis leading downhill from the Hall of Languages. This construction marked the first time campus structures formally crossed University Place. It was also the start of a romance with Beaux-Arts principles that the University would embrace for decades to come. In vogue between 1895 and 1920, Beaux-Arts style was a style characterized by grand interior and exterior columns, large windows, and ornate entryways.

THE 1906 MASTER PLAN

During the first decade of his term, Chancellor Day doubled the size of the campus and added four new buildings. With no master plan to draw on, expansion continued impetuously, and so the administration sought new planning efforts. In 1905 *The Onondagan* sponsored a design competition for twenty alumni architects. Although the winning scheme was never used, a 1906 design by Syracuse architecture professors Frederick Revels and Earl Hallenbeck was adopted by the Day administration.

Revels and Hallenbeck sought to bring an orderly sequence to chaotic university building patterns. In attempting to reshape the existing campus, their plan focused on the Old Oval. It proposed defining the south side of the field with new buildings parallel to the Old Row, thereby reshaping it into the Great Quadrangle. To the west, the architects also sited a stadium in a shallow ravine, allowing the Oval to become a ceremonial green space.

The plan's most remarkable feature was culled from *The Onondagan*: a domed addition to the rear of the Hall of Languages. Intended to hold an assembly hall, this addition would have remade the Hall of Languages into the north wing of a massive structure extending south along the edge of the Old Oval. However, it was never built.

To landscape the campus Revels and Hallenbeck hired Frederick L. Olmstead, Jr., son of renowned landscape architect Frederick Olmstead, Sr., who designed Manhattan's Central Park and Prospect Park in Brooklyn. One design was accepted but never realized.

When Chancellor Day supported the 1906 plan, Revels and Hallenbeck received more commissions. Many of their buildings between 1904 and 1921 were designed in Beaux-Arts modified by a common Renaissance motif. Carnegie Library (1907), Bowne Hall (1907), Sims Hall (1907), Archbold Stadium (1908), and Archbold Gymnasium (1909) quickly completed the south side of the Great Quadrangle. Slocum Hall was added in 1918.

Aerial view of the Revels and Hallenbeck Plan, 1906. Note the two dormitories, Winchell and Haven Halls, at the crossing of University Place and University Avenue. Both have been torn down. Courtesy of Syracuse University Archives

10. *Carnegie Library, 1907*

Cost: $300,000
Architects: Revels and Hallenbeck, Syracuse
Builders: Dawson Brothers, Syracuse

In 1905 millionaire philanthropist Andrew Carnegie surprised the University with $150,000 to construct a library bearing his name, one of several academic libraries funded by him in the early twentieth century. To receive the gift, the University had to match the grant; the school had to raise an equal amount as endowment for the library's maintenance. It took a scant month for the sum to be raised, and the new library, with gray brick, terra-cotta, and granite façade and sweeping Beaux-Arts stairway, became an instant architectural asset. For many years Carnegie Library would serve as the main library on campus. Today it houses collections from the Department of Mathematics and from science and technology-related departments.

Carnegie Library at SU is one of eight original Carnegie libraries still in use on a college campus.

Carnegie Library reading room. Courtesy of Syracuse University Archives

11. *Sims Hall, 1907*

Architects: Revels and Hallenbeck, Syracuse
Renovation and addition: 1989-91; Architects: Office of Design
and Construction, Syracuse University, Syracuse

Leftover moneys from the Carnegie funding effort made construction of Sims Hall possible. Built of reinforced concrete faced with pale, veined marble, red brick, and terra-cotta, Sims Hall was the first male residence on campus. The building was named after Charles N. Sims, third chancellor of Syracuse University. The original structure draws particular strength from an angled corner entrance framed by elegant pillars added in the 1991 renovation. Five distinctly identifiable vertical entrances led to units housed under one common roof, including dining and lounge facilities. This design was a response to substantial resistance from the University community to the "dorm" concept, which signaled a departure from traditional "cottage" housing for students. Ironically, by the 1960s Sims Hall would need a sixth entrance as part of a conversion to quarters for the School of Social Work in order to legitimize it as home for an academic unit.

Eventually, the building would serve other aspects of University life. For a while it contained the engineering program. A later dining hall addition was remodeled into the Joe and Emily Lowe Gallery. Sims Hall houses varied classrooms and offices including the Department of Public Safety, Department of Communication and Rhetorical Studies, Department of African American Studies, and the Martin Luther King, Jr., Memorial Library.

Sims Hall. Courtesy of Syracuse University Archives

12. *Bowne Hall, 1907*

Cost: $175,000 (approximate)
Architects: Revels and Hallenbeck, Syracuse
Builders: Dawson Brothers, Syracuse

Bowne Hall was meant to provide new quarters for the Department of Chemistry, which had outgrown cramped space in the basement of the Hall of Languages. It was originally called Bowne Hall of Chemistry and was made completely fireproof. In time, ivy scampered across its red brick exterior. Classroom desks of red oak evoke the warmth of the past, as do hallway floors of red concrete. The building was named for early trustee Samuel Bowne, who contributed $100,000 toward its completion. Today this neoclassic landmark hosts the Graduate School and various programs of the College of Arts and Sciences.

Another building erected the same year as Bowne Hall (1907) was Archbold Stadium, designed by Revels and Hallenbeck and built on the site now occupied by the Carrier Dome. Archbold Stadium was razed in 1978 to make way for the Dome. When built, Archbold was the largest concrete stadium in the country and the third in the United States constructed with reinforced concrete.

It may be hard to believe but sports at Syracuse University got off to a shaky start. The first gym was a shabby shed barely visible in back of the Hall of Languages. Athletes shared it with the school janitor and occasional intruding chickens from an adjacent coop. On April 12, 1886, several appalled athletes allegedly burned the place to a cinder after the chancellor's cow wandered in. One student diary of the day suggested that freshmen were not only "prodded by the sophomores to do the job" but were also encouraged by two SU professors who had often said that they "hoped the old shed would catch fire and burn down." [12]

A *real* gymnasium was finally built in 1892 on the site of the present Hendricks Chapel. Modern twentieth-century athletic facilities would follow, starting with the aforementioned Archbold Stadium (1907) and Archbold Gymnasium and culminating in the Carrier Dome (1980) (see page 110) and Flanagan Gym (1989) (see page 118).

Bowne Hall. Courtesy of Syracuse University Archives

Archbold Stadium with construction of Archbold Gymnasium in the foreground, ca. 1908. Courtesy of Syracuse University Archives

Bowne Hall, Carnegie Library, and Archbold Gymnasium. Courtesy of Syracuse University Archives

13. *Archbold Gymnasium, 1908*

Cost: $175,000 (approximate)
Architects: Revels and Hallenbeck, Syracuse
Renovation and addition: 1952; Architect: Lorimer Rich,
  New York, N.Y.

Conceived as an annex to Archbold Stadium, this gymnasium became a reality when benefactor John D. Archbold paid off a university debt to guarantee its construction. Archbold was chairman of the Board of Trustees of Syracuse University, president of Standard Oil of New Jersey, and a good friend to Chancellor Day. A man of considerable wealth and social station, he was also a major donor on almost every project constructed during Day's term. In 1947 the worst fire in University history devastated the gymnasium that bore his name, leaving only the outer walls of the original structure. University architect Lorimer Rich remodeled the gym as late as 1952. Rich also designed an addition with swimming pools. Prior to the disaster, the swimming pool was located under what is now the Bursar's Office.

Writer Upton Sinclair observed that Chancellor Day was, during his term (1894–1922), wildly committed to "expanding the university . . . and fending off the evils of socialism."[13] Day's vision propelled a building frenzy in 1907. Soon the silhouettes of Machinery Hall and Lyman Hall towered above the Lawn in dramatic counterpoint to the Old Row extension. As a pedestrian turns into College Place, Lyman Hall extends the Old Row along University Place while firmly anchoring the west end of campus. At its northeast corner the building footprint is not at right angles. This design was not a planning error; rather, it was skewed to be parallel to both University Place and College Place.

14. *Machinery Hall,* 1907

Cost: $40,000
Architects: Gaggin & Gaggin, Syracuse

A reinforced concrete and steel frame, rocky stone facing, and tile roof give Machinery Hall a rustic air befitting its intent. Shortly after opening, machine shops were moved in from Lyman C. Smith Hall. This was the second engineering building to be gifted by Smith, and the huge loading capacity of its floor (about 500 pounds) was also used to store heavy machinery. After Smith's sudden death in 1910, his widow and son donated a well-equipped hydraulic laboratory in his memory. College of Applied Science professor Paul Nugent designed the lab. One can see photos of Machinery Hall in its early days displayed on the second floor of the building. In 1948, the college moved to Thompson Road, after which Machinery Hall served as a classroom building. Its future use would prove diverse. In 1951 the second floor was home to the SU Drama Department and Boar's Head Theatre. The following year it was further renovated into headquarters for the University ROTC program. In 1964 Machinery Hall became the university computing center. Eventually, a sizeable boiler house to the south was torn down to make way for the construction of Link Hall (see page 104).

Machinery Hall. Courtesy of Syracuse University Archives

15. *Lyman Hall,* 1907

Cost: $250,000
Architects: Revels and Hallenbeck, Syracuse

Trustee John C. Lyman bequeathed this building to the University in memory of his two deceased daughters. When it opened as the Lyman Hall of Natural History, it was occupied by the Departments of Biology, Botany, and Geology. In 1930 the top story was remodeled into a Natural History Museum. Seven years later fire destroyed the entire roof and upper floor, along with a large proportion of the museum's considerable contents. Damage at the time was estimated at $79,000.

With its classic red brick façade, Indiana limestone trim, and gracious windows, Lyman Hall is no doubt the finest example of the Beaux-Arts style on campus. Note the rooftop tower, a scaled-down version of the Roman Temple of Venus, 300 A.D., at Baalbeck (now Lebanon). Local papers called the main entrance a "rare work of art." Critic Montgomery Schuyler, however, blasted Revels and Hallenbeck's design for "outrageous self-complacency and aggressiveness" and "excessive pretentiousness." Yet its classic presence has weathered the test of time. Interior oak woodwork, ornamental balustrades, and elaborate mosaic floors recall craftsmanship and refinements of a bygone era. The double front entrance stair was restored to its original materials and design in 2002–2003. Today Lyman Hall houses a number of biology offices.

Perhaps the most lasting effect of the 1906 Plan was the strengthening of two seminal campus open spaces. Revels and Hallenbeck had modified and formalized the Old Oval into a Main Quadrangle meant to bring new order to campus. They also called for an eastward extension of the Old Row and Lawn paving the way for a new generation of buildings along the crest of the Hill.

In a variety of ways the 1906 Plan offered a surprisingly loose interpretation of Beaux-Arts principles. While Revels and Hallenbeck planned most of the resultant buildings, their individual designs never quite found an overall architectural vision. The University's penchant for eclecticism continued, contrary to architectural conventions of the day—and critics were unsparing.

Lyman Hall

Montgomery Schuyler, writing for *The Architectural Record,* said of the Syracuse campus in 1911: "Here was ample room to lay out a collection of buildings which should have an effect of unity in the aggregate, together with whatever variety their varying purposes might invite or permit in detail. And seemingly there has been enough money spent on buildings to execute such a scheme handsomely and impressively. The actual result is simply deplorable in the crudity of the parts and the absence of anything that can be decently called a whole. There is, it seems, a course of architecture at Syracuse, which will fail of its purpose unless it inculcates upon its students the primary necessity of refraining from doing anything like the buildings of the campus." [14]

WORLD WAR I

James Roscoe Day often expressed a pronounced dislike of military plans and training camps, yet he guided the University through two historic international conflicts, the Spanish American War (1898) and World War I (1916–18).

At the dawn of the Great War, Chancellor Day had the dubious distinction of being barred from his own campus by an armed guard patrolling a student training troop. At the height of the war, he told students that "It is religious to hate the German Kaiser. After all," he said, "the Bible teaches us to hate the devil." [15]

During wartime, Syracuse, like other universities across the nation, became what was called a "full-fledged military institution." [16] A mess hall was assembled behind Sims Dormitory. Fraternity houses were turned into army barracks. At least one thousand students enlisted. Enrollment dropped by 30 percent.

Announcing that "Hell is too good for young men unwilling to serve," Day demanded that the ROTC (Reserved Officers Training Corps) come to the University, an act that would cause him no end of political irritation.

Despite Chancellor Day's powerful record of university expansion, SU found itself on financially shaky ground. No more buildings would rise on campus until Slocum Hall was erected in 1918.

16. *Slocum Hall, 1918*

Cost: $400,000
Architect: Earl Hallenbeck, Syracuse
Builders: Dawson Brothers, Syracuse

Mrs. Russell Sage had financed Slocum Hall for the University's Department of Agriculture in memory of her father, Joseph H. Slocum, a pioneer in agricultural education and former state senator from Onondaga County.

At its inception Slocum Hall was well placed at the former turnaround site of the Euclid Avenue Trolley.

Slocum Hall was designed in 1915 and slated to open in 1917. However, construction was delayed due to stormy labor conditions and America's entry into World War I. When finally completed in October 1918, its formal dedication had to be further postponed. This time the University was quarantined because of the Spanish flu epidemic.

Upon opening, Slocum was hailed as "one of the finest structures on the Hill . . . furnished with the most up-to-date appliances."[17] Its grandeur is well served by an imposing exterior of Moosebeck granite and Indiana limestone with pink granite basement and trim. Titanic columns facing College Place flank an elegant main entrance crowned by a balcony.

The original atrium allowed natural light to flood the upper four floors while thick masonry kept the interior warm in winter and cool in summer. The atrium was filled in during the 1960s to provide more floor space. Current renovations call for restoration of the atrium (see pp. 125–26). Over its long history Slocum Hall has housed the Graduate School, Education, Human Development, and Business. The School of Architecture, situated first in Crouse College and Bowne Hall, relocated to Slocum in 1919. When current renovations of Slocum are completed in 2007, the School of Architecture will—for the first time since its founding in 1873—occupy an entire building by itself.

Slocum Hall

THE JAZZ AGE

The Roaring Twenties ushered in an era of prosperity, social change, and unshakable confidence. Like the rest of the nation, students on the Hill seemed bent on having a good time. Dating often meant a short trolley ride downtown for dinner and a silent movie at the Rivoli or Eckel. Coeds and their beaus kicked up their heels with abandon, until Chancellor Day laid down the law—no cigarettes and no dancing two weeks before the end of semester. "We are close upon examination," he said, "and have no time to dance." [18]

His severe demeanor notwithstanding, Day's twenty-eight-year tenure produced remarkable results for the University. Enrollment grew from less than seven hundred students to over six thousand. Twenty-four new buildings were erected and eleven colleges were founded, including the School of Forestry (later to become SUNY-ESF) that he somehow wooed away from Cornell.

17. *Robin Hood Oak*

On the grounds at SUNY-ESF, one comes upon a fabled campus site. Around 1926 Professor C. Brown brought to Syracuse an acorn from the famous major oak of England's Sherwood Forest. Brown planted it near Bray Hall, and from that tiny acorn an oak tree grew tall and strong. It has come to be called the Robin Hood Oak.

Robin Hood Oak

THE GREEKS HAD
A WORD FOR IT

During the heady 1920s the Highlands District, north of University Place, kept on growing, but its disposition was changing. As early as the 1900s, fraternities and sororities began retreating from Irving Avenue. Gradually, Greek Letter houses displaced those of the original homeowners, spelling the area's demise as a fashionable district.

It was no accident that college fraternities gained favor in the preceding Victorian era. Education at that time was a rigid matter, and Greek societies provided welcome opportunities for friendship, frolic, and meaningful endeavor. The first fraternity at SU was Delta Kappa Epsilon, founded in 1871. Within short time others followed.

Female students, expressing similar needs, yearned for "something of their own," only to face derision by their male counterparts. In 1872 twelve brave young women at Syracuse University founded Alpha Phi, one of the first sororities in the nation. Unaware that several similar organizations were springing up elsewhere in the country, they held clandestine meetings in a leased space in downtown Syracuse. Outraged male students later termed the group "a secret society . . . of the ladies of the lower class."[19] Not to be daunted, these plucky femmes kept alive what were then called "women fraternities."[20]

As a matter of fact the word sorority first entered the English language at Syracuse University in 1874. Based on the Latin *soror* for "sister," it was coined for the newborn Gamma Phi Beta Society by their advisor, Dr. Frank Smalley, who felt the word fraternity unbecoming to young ladies.

The 1920s were palmy days for Greek Letter societies. Flush with money, fraternities and sororities built grand new houses around the perimeter of Walnut Park. By World War II that same city park had, by default, become part and parcel of Syracuse University.

Walnut Park is still lined with Greek chapter houses. As outlined by Eva-Maria Hardin in *Syracuse Landmarks,* a walk through the area offers a rewarding glimpse at the stately architecture of a bygone era, notably:

18. *310 Walnut Place, ca. 1925*

Graceful symmetry defines this grand Neoclassical Revival, originally built for Sigma Phi Epsilon fraternity. One of its most imposing features is a classical entrance porch reaching the complete height but not the width of the house and a central open-topped doorway. The building is now home to the Suskind Center of International Affairs.

19. *308 Walnut Place, 1898*

Before becoming the Alpha Phi sorority house, this fine Colonial started out as a private residence. Note the five-bay façade, stepped gables, brick-faced end walls, striking garret windows, and handsome Federal door. A leaded glass fanlight is inset with the sorority emblem.

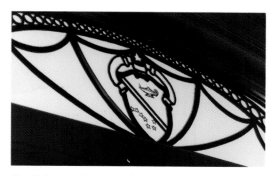

Fanlight over the front door at 308 Walnut Place

20. *306 Walnut Place, 1928*

Architect: Marjorie Wright, Syracuse

Here one finds a quintessential Tudor house with entrance surrounded by stone tabs, mock half-timbering, and steep gables. It was built as a sorority house for Kappa Alpha Theta, of which Marjorie Wright was a member. Wright worked for her father, prominent local architect Gordon A. Wright.

The Tudor front of 306 Walnut Place

21. *304 Walnut Place, 1899*

Architect: Gordon A. Wright, Syracuse

This Colonial Revival was designed for George Larrabee, manager of the National Biscuit Company. Prominent garrets and chimneys are distinguishing features. Shell motifs adorn the windows while Ionic columns line the front porch.

Shell motif on window frames at 304 Walnut Place

22. *300 Walnut Place, 1903*

Addition: ca. 1923

It is not so much the grandeur of this Georgian Revival but its intent that affirms the privileged status of old Walnut Park. Its original owners, the Denison family, built the house solely for purposes of entertainment. Tri Delta sorority added a Doric portico for that "Greek touch" when they purchased it twenty years later.

Stately columns at 300 Walnut Place

23. *901 Walnut Avenue, 1907*

Addition: 1940s

First erected as a private residence, 901 Walnut Avenue now hosts the Delta Gamma sorority. Few alterations were made to its Tudor Revival front over the years, although a side wing and enclosed side porch were added in the 1940s.

24. *210 Walnut Place, 1897*

Renovations: 1923

A prime example of Colonial Revival architecture built for noted local clergyman, Bishop Huntington. The structure became a social club for men before serving as the Phi Beta Phi sorority house.

25. *200 Walnut Place, ca. 1900*

Designed as a dwelling for Reverend E. McChesney, this residence ultimately became the Colonial Revival and originally housed the Kappa Phi Delta fraternity. It is now the SU Counseling Center. Note its hipped roof, prominent dormers, and symmetrically expressed Ionic columns.

26. *705 Walnut Avenue*

Architect: William H. Miller, Ithaca, N.Y.

Faced in Roman brick and topped by a tile roof, this mansion was built for Albert E. Nettleton, founder of A. E. Nettleton Company, famous shoe manufacturers in Syracuse. An impressive semicircular porch and six-sided towers front on Walnut Park. Today the building houses the Alpha Chi Omega sorority.

Albert E. Nettleton later became president of the Paragon Plaster Company. His Nettleton shoe factory in downtown Syracuse has been converted into modern apartments.

705 Walnut Avenue

27. *703 Walnut Avenue,* 1905

Architects: Gaggin & Gaggin, Syracuse
Renovation and partial restoration: 1988; Architects: Crawford &
  Stearns, Syracuse

Designed for Horace S. Wilkinson, founder and chairman of the board of the Crucible Steel Company, 703 Walnut Avenue has been home to Delta Kappa Epsilon fraternity since the mid-twentieth century. Elegant proportions and a stone front lend a palatial ambience. A steep, tiled roof along with gables, towers, turrets, and battlement porches echo the stylistic flamboyance of the day. Interior woodwork is offset by an intricately carved walnut staircase, and there is a room completely done in Moorish fashion.

President Theodore Roosevelt once spent a night at 703 Walnut Avenue as guest of the Wilkinsons during the Barnes-Wilkinson libel suit (1915).

28. *Chancellor's Residence, 1901 701 Walnut Avenue*

Architects: Benson & Brockway, Syracuse

Situated on two acres bounded by Comstock Avenue, Harrison Street, and Walnut Park, this mansion was built as a residence for local attorney and University trustee William Nottingham. Made of Indiana limestone trimmed with red and black brick, the twenty-two room house features colossal entry arches and steep gables as well as prominent dormers and chimneys. Inside one finds rich English and Canadian oak, elaborate fireplaces, and a library with leather-lined walls. A carved central staircase curves up three stories to a grand ballroom that is no longer in use.

> *Fourteen years after the Nottinghams moved into their magnificent home, they offered to "trade" it for the more modest Chancellor's residence at 604 University Avenue plus some additional cash.*

Other Walnut Park buildings of architectural interest, as noted in *Syracuse Landmarks,* are located at the historically intact juncture of Walnut Avenue and Madison Street. Both present handsome Tudor fronts. Both were designed by Ward Wellington Ward.

29. *519 Walnut Avenue, 1911*

Built as a residence for Herbert Walker, now an apartment house.

30. *604 Walnut Avenue, 1910*

Built for Samuel Cook, No. 604 is also used as an apartment house, with an additional entrance at 920 Madison Avenue.

The Madison Avenue entrance to 604 Walnut Avenue

31. *John G. Alibrandi, Jr., Catholic Center, ca. 1899*

110–112 Walnut Place

Addition: 1982; Architects: Hueber, Hares, & Glavin, Syracuse

Considerable renovation turned this private home into the St. Thomas More Chapel. Through a generous a gift of the Alibrandi family, a modern addition resulted in the Catholic Center. At the middle of the new chapel one finds the Center's Reservation Chapel, which can be entered from the main entrance hall. A folding oak panel partition opens onto the St. Thomas More Chapel. Within the addition there are offices, a multiuse room, and kitchen. An open loggia near the main entry to the Center itself creates a small courtyard melding both new and old into a uniform scale.

Two distinctive Greek Life houses survive near Walnut Park: Psi Upsilon House, at the corner of College and University Places, and Goldstein Alumni Center, directly across the street. Each is an outstanding example of Neoclassical Revival architecture.

Alibrandi Catholic Center. Courtesy of Syracuse University Archives

32. *Psi Upsilon,* 1898

Architect: Wellington Taber

Psi Upsilon was the first structure on campus to be built specifically as a frater-nity house. Two majestic porticoes flank its entrance, and an octagonal cupola and classic detail create an aura of grandeur distinctive to mansions of its type and time. Architect Wellington Taber (1866–1943) was a member of Psi Upsilon and a graduate of the School of Architecture at SU.

> *Psi Upsilon House is listed on the National Register of Historic Places.*

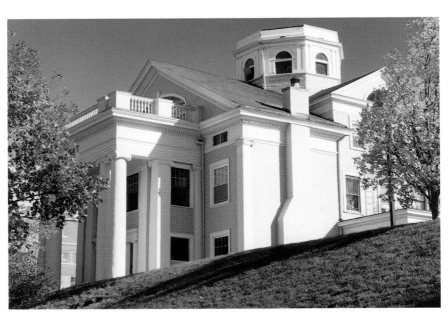

Psi Upsilon. Courtesy of Bohlin Cywinski Jackson

33. *Goldstein Alumni and Faculty Center, 1903*

Architects: Gaggin & Gaggin, Syracuse

When fraternity brothers of Delta Kappa Epsilon opened this Modified Federal style structure, they billed it as "the newest and finest chapter house at Syracuse." Passersby are still impressed by its three-story façade of red Akron brick with bay windows, sills, and trimmings of pure white Vermont marble. The building foundation is made of Onondaga limestone. Kaleidoscopic stained glass windows look onto elegant interiors of rich oak, paneled walls, and beamed ceilings.

Over the years 401 University Place has had many incarnations. Like other fraternity houses it served as temporary living quarters for GIs after World War II. SU bought the structure when Delta Kappa Epsilon moved on to new quarters in 1974. Refurbished as a faculty center, it became a favorite gathering spot for faculty, staff, and students to meet, sip coffee, and engage in lively discussion. The Office of Alumni Relations was added in 1996.

Goldstein Alumni and Faculty Center

THE 1928 MASTER PLAN

Construction on campus went into decline after James Roscoe Day left in 1922. Yet the ongoing quest to refine the university environment led, in the 1920s, to the next comprehensive campus plan. Chancellor Flint announced that New York City architects John Russell Pope and Dwight James Baum had been engaged to create a "harmonizing plan for new buildings, exterior alteration of those already standing and extensive campus landscaping."

The choice of architects signified the high caliber and ambitious scope of the new plan. "Pope had designed many buildings which, through robust

Aerial view of North Campus, late 1920s. Courtesy of Syracuse University Archives

68

commitment to classicism and strong axial organization, have come to typify official Washington, D.C. Baum, a graduate of the Syracuse architecture program, was known as a champion of Georgian Revival residential design." [21] Together, they developed an impressive fifty-year master plan that used the existing campus as a foundation. Like their predecessors they sought a physical environment that was aesthetically pleasing yet ordered.

Pope and Baum's cohesive vision for the campus consciously rejected prior and present eclecticism. It was a grand Beaux-Arts plan unified by neo-Georgian buildings that would give the campus shape and extend it into the neighborhoods beyond.

Their design called for groups of like academic disciplines to be placed around a series of quadrangles. A domed chapel would bisect the Old Oval, creating smaller twin quads. The College of Forestry (now SUNY-ESF) was to occupy a third quad. An expanded medical center would rise across Irving

Rendering from an aerial perspective of the Pope-Baum campus plan. Note the proposed auditorium annexed to Hendricks Chapel. Courtesy of Syracuse University Archives

Avenue while a number of cross axes were meant to extend north into the street at University Hill.

For the centerpiece, Pope and Baum resurrected an idea from the 1906 plan. This called for an extremely large assembly hall as new focal point for the academic core. They struck an east-west axis through the two existing quadrangles and placed a new structure at its heart. All of which would require moving the Old Gymnasium.

To the west of the assembly hall the architects conceived a monumental stairway spilling down the steep hillside. Bordered by new buildings aligned with the Old Row, the grand stair would create an imposing symbolic gateway to the University from Irving Avenue.

The 1928 Pope-Baum Plan was the most detailed and comprehensive campus design ever attempted by the University. It was, said Chancellor Flint, "the most momentous undertaking the university has ever adopted." [22]

The architects' first steps called for the construction of Hendricks Chapel and Maxwell Hall. Plans were grand. Hopes were great. Once again, external events would exact a price.

THE GREAT DEPRESSION

Soon after the Pope-Baum Plan was disclosed, SU trustees hired professional fundraisers. In 1929 a major campaign was approved. Ten days later the stock market crashed, devastating at once the nation's economy and spirit. Universities were not spared.

"The Great Depression had brought a rude end to the genteel social and economic circumstances that had enabled academic institutions to pursue visions of a well-ordered future."[23] Within two years, by 1931, fundraising efforts were suspended.

The Pope-Baum Plan withered. Hendricks Chapel was constructed in 1930, but its vast companion assembly hall never materialized. Fragments of the Academic, Medical, and Forestry Groups were built. Both Dormitory Groups lived only on paper. University Avenue remained the traditional approach to the Hill. The great stair of Irving Avenue, envisioned as the University's western gateway, would never come to be.

Only two buildings from the Pope-Baum Plan were added to the core campus during the 1930s: Hendricks Chapel and Maxwell Hall.

34. *Hendricks Chapel, 1930*

Cost: $600,000
Architects: John Russell Pope and Dwight James Baum,
    New York, N.Y.
Builder: A. E. Stephens Company, Springfield, Mass.

From the outset, the Chapel opened its doors to people of all faiths. Greek and Roman themes employed throughout created a space that evoked the spirit of sanctuary yet was devoid of specific religious symbol. Basic design motifs were drawn from the octagon, the circle, and the Greek cross. One sees these in neoclassic interior ornamentation, skylight shape, and occasional window spacing. Colonial seats and a pulpit were gifts the Class of 1918. Made of brick and limestone structure in Georgian Revival style, the chapel recalls classic Jeffersonian aesthetics. Its steel-framed, lead-covered dome forges a focal point between two commanding quadrangles. Colossal steps lead to a timeless portico with fluted ionic columns.

Hendricks was, at the time of its construction, the third-largest chapel in the country with a seating capacity of 1,450.

Former Syracuse mayor and University trustee Francis Hendricks built the chapel in memory of his wife, Eliza Jane. But upon completion in September 1930, there were no funds for an organ. Thanks to the generosity of Kathryn Hendricks, the mayor's niece, an Aeolian organ was installed a month later.

Fifty-five years later, on September 22, 1985, Hendricks Chapel was rededicated to honor the completion of a five-year $1.2 million restoration plan. Various religious groups still use Hendricks for worship, special services, lectures, convocations, and weddings.

Hendricks Chapel. Courtesy of Syracuse University Archives

35. *Maxwell School of Citizenship and Public Affairs, 1937*

Architects: John Russell Pope and Dwight James Baum, New York, N.Y.

Renovation and expansion: 1994; Architects: Bohlin Cywinski Jackson, Wilkes-Barre, Pa.

George Holmes Maxwell was a successful attorney and entrepreneur whose passion was what he called "intelligent patriotism." On October 3, 1924 he opened the Maxwell School of Citizenship and Public Affairs with six graduate students in public administration. Its mission was to train "teachers of citizenship" and "practitioners of public affairs." The original school was lodged on the second floor of Slocum Hall but quickly outgrew that space.

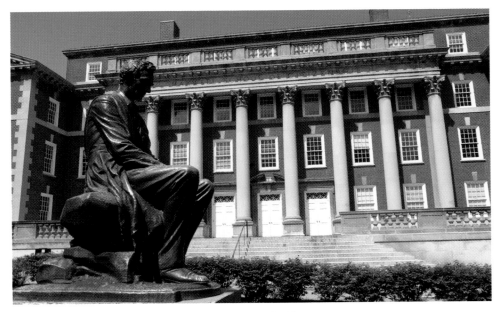

Maxwell Hall. Courtesy of Syracuse University Archives

Although financed in 1929 by Maxwell and his wife, Carrie A. Maxwell, the *new* Maxwell Hall was not part of the Pope-Baum Plan of 1927. As noted earlier, that plan called for a Georgian Revival style structure at the Irving Avenue entrance fronted by a majestic staircase and a pathway of colonnades. Conceding to the wishes of the chancellor and donors, the University placed Maxwell I, as it came to be known, between the Administration Building and Crouse College. On one hand this choice weakened the architectural dynamic between the two buildings. On the other, its arcade with monumental columns did create a grand entrance off Crouse Avenue.

Dedication ceremonies for Maxwell were held at Hendricks Chapel on November 12, 1937. Former President Herbert C. Hoover was principal speaker. Perhaps the building's most striking feature is the main entrance lobby. A towering antechamber with Ionic columns and dark terrazzo floors, it holds a fitting replica of Jean-Antoine Houdon's life-size statue of George Washington and a wall inscription of the Athenian oath of citizenship.

In 1990, Maxwell School mounted a $50-million expansion so that it

Washington and the Athenian quote, Maxwell Hall. Courtesy of Syracuse University Archives

could offer more extensive programs, professorships, scholarships, and the like. On May 2, 1992, ground was broken for what would become the Maxwell Complex of today. From the start, the goal was to forge an "integrated social science complex." Located in the heart of the historic core campus, the newly designed Eggers Hall, built in 1993, was joined to the old Maxwell Hall. Under the new construction project, the older Maxwell received a complete renovation. The 1937 building is listed on the National Register of Historic Places.

36. *Abraham Lincoln, 1930*

This powerful bronze sculpture stands in the East Court between Maxwell and the Administration Building. Cast especially for the University, it was set in its current place in 1968. Sculptor James Earle Fraser also designed the U.S. buffalo nickel. Another one of his works, depicting the young Lincoln, can be seen at the SUNY-ESF campus just south of Archbold Gymnasium.

Architects Pope and Baum never did see their plan realized; yet the spirit of their vision informs the modern campus. Their design for a main quadrangle with Hendricks Chapel at its core came to be, and a sequence of quads, as inspired by them, would characterize future campus plans. "The architects also created varied north-south axes across the Lawn that joined the Old Row with two proposed dormitories north of University Place. Stitching the campus into the surrounding urban fabric, these north-south axes would remain one of the plan's most compelling design legacies." [24]

WORLD WAR II

At the outset of the Second World War (1942), Syracuse had a population of 205,967, making it the forty-first most populous city in the nation. That same year the draft was extended to eighteen-year-olds. One-half of the reserves on campus were called up. One-third of the student body would enter the armed forces.

Thousands of servicemen also came to the University to enroll in on-campus training detachments of the Army Air Corps and in the Army and Navy Medical Corps.

For the duration of the war, the city of Syracuse and the University were hubs of patriotic activity. Changes to campus life ranged from the mundane to the profound. Slocum Hall was turned into a PX for the Army. The Chapel Association sold war bonds. Sports for the 1943–44 school year were canceled due to transportation difficulties. Intercollegiate athletics were postponed altogether for the duration. Paper shortages caused *The Daily Orange* to publish only four times a week instead of five.

By war's end 18,000 alumni and SU students were in uniform. Reported killed: 195. Missing: 51. Six SU grads earned the private service cross; 426 won other medals of varied distinction.

With young men dwindling in number during the war, the wartime coed found herself in an unprecedented position. Like women across the country she was being primed for jobs traditionally relegated to men. With training in air raid transportation, home nursing, and mechanics, women on campus were turned into collegiate "Rosie the Riveters." For the first time, in 1944, an all-woman staff took charge of *The Daily Orange*. A shortage of nurses at home and overseas led to the opening of the School of Nursing on June 25, 1943. Cadet nurses began to appear. They lived at first in scattered cottages on campus, then in several other locations. In 1973 the School of Nursing purchased the Delta Upsilon fraternity house at 426 Ostrom Avenue. It stayed there until its demise in June 2006. The building now houses the College of Human Services and Health Professions.

37. *426 Ostrom Avenue*

Architect: Gordon Schopfer
Builder: Earl W. Schopfer

Situated high on a hill across from Thornden Park, the former Delta Upsilon house is a two-story whitewashed brick on a stone foundation with a long rear extension of natural brick. Fluted porticoes flank its broad porch while a classic colonial door faces the Park. In one of the large first floor meeting rooms one can still see the Delta Upsilon crest inset on the brick wall above the fireplace mantel.

Stephen Crane was a member of Delta Upsilon. He wrote the first draft of **Maggie: A Girl of the Streets** *at the original Ostrom Avenue fraternity house.*

An elegant Victorian mansion preceded the current structure. Built in 1875 for Dr. Wellesley P. Coddington, a professor of philosophy at SU, the building was bought by Delta Upsilon in 1887. One fraternity brother called it a "commodious residence." [25] It also had the distinction of being the oldest physical structure in the country to be used as a fraternity house. In 1955 Delta Upsilon razed it to build anew. And Coddington's glorious mansion took its place on the vanished campus.

Professor Coddington's mansion, ca. 1875. Courtesy of the Onondaga Historical Association

THE POSTWAR ERA

After World War II the University began to build again, largely in response to an explosive upsurge in enrollment. Majestic Beaux-Arts aesthetics so rapturously employed only two decades earlier were discarded by leading campus designers. Colleges were facing uncharted terrain in higher education amid a nation beset by change.

> *By September 1946, veterans found themselves housed in everything from cavernous structures on a Mattydale army base to a series of converted animal stalls at the State Fair Grounds.*

For the first time in America's history vast numbers of citizens from diverse economic and ethnic backgrounds were able to attend a university. Prime among these were thousands of servicemen returning from war. Under the GI bill, which provided tuition, room and board, and a small stipend, they came to prepare for new and, it was hoped, better civilian lives.

During wartime 12,706 young men had come to SU for special training. Embraced by the city, several thousand came back to study after the war. Of the eight thousand SU students who served in the armed forces, six thousand would return to the school. Postwar universities were often not welcoming to such disruption. SU was an exception—with good reason. The University entered this new era still reeling from the effects of debt, the Great Depression, and war.

The *Syracuse University Campus Plan 2003* points out that "the concurrent surge in enrollment represented an opportunity for transformation. New York was unusual among large industrialized states because it lacked a strong public 'land-grant' University system."[26] Guided by Chancellor William P. Tolley, Syracuse stepped aggressively into the breach to absorb the flood of new students. Registration doubled to 12,000, peaking at 15,000 by 1948.

Such unprecedented enrollment numbers plunged SU into a stunning struggle between explosive growth and adequate construction. Consequences for the present and future campus would be deep and long lasting as earlier, grand visions of Beaux-Arts architecture fell by the wayside in deference to urgent housing needs. Postwar University planners worked under extreme pressure. Theirs was an ideal fueled by the belief that enrollment would pursue a limitless upward trajectory. In retrospect they made a number of political and planning mistakes.

At first financial constraints excluded permanent physical expansion of the campus. Immediate space demands were of the essence. In 1946 the university bought 175 trailers from the Navy. Placed in a DeWitt apple orchard called Mud Hollow, these provided temporary living quarters for one hundred married couples without children.

As the need for more space arose, the University set up additional housing, also for married students, in the area that would become Skytop or South Campus. Twenty-five prefabs purchased from war workers in Massena served

Mud Hollow trailers. Courtesy of Syracuse University Archives

as lodging for more families, and the Yates Hotel opened parts of two floors for student residential use.

Other emergency sites were devised. In the end Syracuse put up the largest class of veterans in New York State. So impressed was Governor Thomas Dewey that he sold 700 prefabricated military buildings, called Quonset huts, to the University for one dollar each.

The land behind Hendricks Chapel filled rapidly with prefabs intended for academic use. Temporary residential "cities" rose on what became the Manley Field House area, and on the grounds of the University Farm at what is now Skytop. A prefab dining hall called the Quonseteria became the new "town" center. It was a graceless beginning to the school's greatest period of expansion. Yet, as academic finances improved, the University would begin to build in a manner befitting its newfound size and status.

In 1948 university landscape architect Noreda Rotunno unveiled the first of several designs intended to handle future population growth and university

Quonset huts on main campus. Courtesy of Syracuse University Archives

expansion. Rotunno planned an "inner liner" of buildings along the Old Row, creating a narrowed Natural Science Quadrangle on the site of the former Old Oval. He also projected a dormitory group for Mount Olympus, along with new residence halls sited to the east and north of the campus core.

Ruthless demolition defined the core of Rotunno's plans. There was no room for sentimentality. The Old Gymnasium had been relocated in 1928 between Steele Hall and Archbold Stadium to make way for Hendricks Chapel. In 1965 it was brought down for a new Physics Building. Even a magnificent landmark like Yates Castle would not be spared.

Walking around Crouse College to Irving Avenue, one comes upon SUNY Upstate Medical University, College of Medicine. It was on this site that Yates Castle (1852–1955) once stood in all its Gothic glory. Clothing manufacturer Cornelius T. Longstreet erected this twenty-four-room replica of a Norman castle for his family. It was first called Renwick Hall after architect James Renwick, who later designed the Smithsonian Institution in Washington, D.C., and St. Patrick's Cathedral in New York City. Built at a cost of $50,000, complete with bridge and moat, the castle looked out over a forty-nine-acre estate at the peak of the Irving Avenue hill.

For the Longstreets, however, Renwick Hall's bucolic setting proved too far from the social whirl of the city. Striking a deal with clothing merchant Alonzo Yates, Cornelius Longstreet traded the castle for Yates's James Street house, plus $30,000, and the castle was renamed for its new owners. Eventually, it went from private home to private institution, Syracuse Classical, then to Slocum Teachers College. In 1934 the new SU School of Journalism moved in. Journalism students called themselves "The Castle Kids."

John North, who carved the castle doors, died on March 11, 1910, in Syracuse. The University has the doors in storage.

Over time SU sold the mansion to its neighbor, the medical college. By the 1950s, the castle was crammed between four hospitals and a medical school, its estate whittled from fourteen to just under two acres. Then the State of New York announced a new wing for the College of Medicine, to be

Yates Castle. Courtesy of Syracuse University Archives

built on the very site of the castle. Ironically, a farewell ball was held on April 25, 1953, with all present dressed in period costume. In 1954 the bulldozers came, and Yates Castle, once the most "glorious local expression of romanticism,"[27] became part of the vanished campus. Still, reminders of the past remain. A ridged stone wall that once bordered the castle can be seen on the west side of Irving Avenue, in front of the Health Sciences Library of SUNY Upstate Medical University. A pair of orange trees planted on the original estate grows on the lawn at Weiskotten Hall. And in August 2005 a construction crew working on the western edge of University Hill unearthed a chunk of concrete. Historians say it is a capstone from a bridge that once arched a ravine at the north end of the original estate.

The deficits of demolition notwithstanding, Rotunno's early efforts drew critical applause. After calling the existing campus "the classic example of hodge-podge in architecture," the *Syracuse Post-Standard* declared that the planner's work showed Syracuse was "at last, after its nearly eighty years, developing an architectural pattern."[28]

"Unlike prior campus planners, Rotunno was able to see many of his projects materialize. The first of Rotunno's bookend buildings for the social science quadrangle, the E. I. White College of Law, was completed in 1954 (p. 88). Construction of the first 'liner' buildings, Hinds Hall (1955, p. 94), H. B. Crouse Hall (1961, p. 91) and Link Hall (1965, p. 104) continued to reduce the size of the Main Quadrangle."[29]

TOLLEY'S BUILDING BULGE

William P. Tolley became seventh chancellor of Syracuse University in 1942. At forty-two he was the youngest chancellor of any university at that time and, as it turned out, one of the most sensitive.

In the course of his twenty-seven-year tenure, Tolley steered the University through significant change and remarkable growth. More than twenty buildings were erected during this era. Tolley's love of literature and books led him to establish Syracuse University Press (1943) and to construct Bird Library (1972, see page 101).

It should be remembered that in 1945 the University was cash poor. With an eye to expansion, Tolley now mounted the school's first serious national development campaign. This initial stage of what would became known as Tolley's "Building Bulge" set out to raise $15 million dollars. After a decade of ups and downs, the new Building and Development Fund reached its goal. Twelve million dollars went into construction, the rest to scholarships and endowments.

Expansion at this time was more than one chancellor's ambitious vision. It was an imperative; the physical campus was bursting at the seams. As Tolley rallied to the cause, it became clear that he would go down in campus history as the chancellor who built a bigger Syracuse University.

First he purchased land, a giant move for a small university in wartime. Most colleges, fearing a postwar recession, were doing the opposite. Tolley not only wanted to expand the campus, he sought to improve its financial standing. The far-seeing chancellor sensed that land values would rise—and he was right.

By 1946 the University owned all frontage along University Place from Irving Avenue to Walnut, with the exception of the small Corner Store, a dearly loved bookstore and snack bar at South Crouse Avenue and University Place. That store would be brought down in 1964 to make way for Newhouse I (see p. 97). Tolley also acquired parcels of land along Waverly, University, and Ostrom Avenues. How and what he would build, and where, remained to be seen.

Concerned about maintaining design standards, SU trustees appointed a University Design Board in 1947 to "formulate and develop a University Plan." Even so, such politically sensitive issues like parking, classroom needs, and housing demands led to decisions that often flew in the face of good urban planning.

Cranes and derricks, steam shovels and bulldozers appeared on campus in profusion. With growing urgency, the Design Board watched major new buildings of minor aesthetic value threaten to consume the Old Oval. Debate raged over whether or not Tolley's vision would destroy the campus elegant. In the end all agreed that immediate productivity was paramount, long-range beauty secondary. William Tolley's dream of an ever-expanding campus was about to become real brick-and-mortar, solid rivet-and-lime.

Much constructed at this time, that is, the College of Law complex and Huntington Beard Crouse Hall, was based on fulfilling the needs of expanding curricula and booming enrollment. A new design motif was sought, one that would visually marry the new structures and rapidly growing dormitories with existing campus architecture. New York City architect Lorimer Rich (1892–1978) and local associates Harry A. and E. Curtis King utilized materials employed in the older buildings, namely brick facing with limestone trim. Thin concrete canopies defined the entrances, resting on two columns. All had a long, low look with flat roofs. In the end this did not constitute the unifying element that was hoped for. On the contrary, Lorimer's modern buildings added "yet another layer to the architectural collage of the campus."

38. *College of Law Complex,* 1954

Cost: $922,000
Architecs: Lorimer Rich and Associates, New York, N.Y.
Contractor: W. J. Burns Company, Syracuse

Before the construction of White Hall, the College of Law had moved in and out of five different locations within the city of Syracuse. White Hall provided the college with a permanent campus home. Made of reinforced concrete with brick facing and limestone trim, it was the ninth structure to be completed in the University's $15 million postwar construction plan. Positioned on a hill, it comprises two distinct levels, one facing west with four stories, the other east with three stories. The building holds classrooms, a library, faculty and administrative offices, lounges, and practice courtrooms.

The rotunda outside White Hall, College of Law

> *White Hall was named for Ernest I. White, a Syracuse lawyer, businessman, and major contributor to the structure's 1947 fund drive.*

Additions such as Grant Auditorium, Barclay Library, and McNaughton Hall link to White Hall, expanding use and embellishing appearance of the entire law complex. Hilltop views, brick footpaths, and arched walkways and traditional lanterns present a rich time-honored look, offset by a stark stone exterior rotunda.

The Arnold M. Grant Auditorium, *1967*

Cost: $800,000
Architects: Lorimer Rich and Associates, New York, N.Y.
Contractor: R. A. Culotti Construction Company

Grant Auditorium adjoins the southern end of White Hall. Within its three stories, one finds a 400-seat auditorium, two lecture halls, seventeen offices, and extra classroom space. The structure was named for trustee and donor Arnold M. Grant, a graduate of Syracuse University College of Law, Class of 1929.

Barclay Law Library Addition, 1985

Cost: $4.5 million
Architects: Bohlin, Powell, Larkin, and Cywinski, Wilkes-Barre, Pa.

The H. Douglas Barclay Library adjoins the northern end of White Hall. Made of brick and limestone, the two-story structure contains auxiliary classroom and computer space. The library holds 319,000 volumes in print and microfilm, along with 5,000 serial titles and it is named for a former state senator and graduate of SU Law School (Class of 1961). Together with his wife, DeeDee, Barclay donated $1 million toward construction of the library. Renovations cost $4.5 million, including refurbishment of White Hall.

Winifred MacNaughton Hall, 1998

This technologically advanced expansion added an approximate 60,000 gross square feet to the college's existing E. I. White Hall. It features spacious classrooms wired for laptop computers, teaching stations with computer platforms, document cameras, and VCRs. It also houses an expanded admissions suite, a renovated library, a new computer cluster, more court space, and five applied learning centers. MacNaughton is designed to replicate a traditional courthouse, public, or academic building. The third floor offers a law clinic and formal courtroom with a judge's chamber. The fourth floor holds student-activity space, reading rooms, and a circular moot courtroom for classes and intramural competitions. A highlight is the law clinic, where students apply classroom knowledge to situations they will face as real-life lawyers. The clinic contains three interview rooms, including one with a two-way mirror for faculty observation.

39. *Huntington Beard Crouse Hall, 1962*

Cost: $1.6 million
Architects: King & King, Syracuse

Designed to accommodate the growing College of Liberal Arts, Crouse Hall was the largest structure created during Tolley's "building bulge." HBC, as students soon called it, offered four floors of classroom space, seventy-seven offices, and two auditoriums. It is a hub for the University's languages, literature, and linguistics departments. A bronze-and-steel welded sculpture, *The Syracuse Nova* (1961) by Harry Bertoia, hangs from the lobby ceiling.

Huntington Beard Crouse Hall was the first building on campus to be completely air-conditioned.

HBC was a gift of Florence Crouse, widow of Huntington, and the Crouse-Hinds Company Foundation. Mrs. Crouse was an 1899 graduate of SU and a member of the Board of Trustees. Huntington Crouse, a local industrialist, founded the Crouse-Hinds Company with Jesse L. Hinds in 1897.

40. *Sacco & Vanzetti, 1966–67*

Along the eastern wall of HBC can be seen perhaps the most renowned work of art on campus. Here is a three-panel marble and enamel mosaic, based on a Ben Shahn painting, portraying the fate of two Italian immigrants, Sacco and Vanzetti, who were accused and executed for robbery and murder in the 1920s. The charges, felt to be unjust by many, ignited controversy. The mosaic's three panels show Sacco and Vanzetti on a street corner, in handcuffs, and in coffins. Created in Chartres, France, in 1957, the mosaic was brought to Syracuse for installation in 1967.

Panel of Ben Shahn's The Passion of Sacco & Vanzetti *at HBC. Courtesy of Syracuse University Archives*

SCIENCE, RESEARCH, AND ART

World War II spawned a sharp surge in scientific research. Crowds of recent servicemen returned, many eager to be trained in engineering. It was no wonder that the College of Applied Science became the fastest growing school on the postwar campus. The first wave of its students was housed in a former naval war plant on Thompson Road. By 1955 student engineers had their own space in Hinds Hall.

41. *Hinds Hall,* 1955

Cost: $940,000
Architects: King & King, Syracuse
Renovation: 2005-06; Architect: Ashley Mabrow

Hinds Hall was conceived as a facility for the budding College of Engineering, now known as the L. C. Smith College of Engineering and Computer Science. The building was named after William Hinds, former chairman of the Crouse-Hinds Company and a University trustee. It is currently being renovated for the School of Information Studies (see p. 126).

Recognizing science as the wave of the future, Tolley began avidly to court serious research. His instincts paid off. By the end of the 1950s, Syra-

Hinds Hall

cuse University was a preeminent player on the stage of institutional research, ranking twelfth nationally in sponsored research.

Art, along with science, emerged as a sphere of vigorous university growth right after the war. With its progressive curriculum, the postwar School of Art became nationally recognized. Most noteworthy was a ground-breaking Mural Program wherein undergraduate art students worked along-side accomplished muralists.

All this was directly related to the Lowe Art Center, first structure completed under the postwar construction plan. Built in 1952 at a cost of $294,000, the Joe and Emily Lowe Art Center was the first new building on campus since 1937. With its simple red brick and limestone façade offset by glass to the north and south sides, the Lowe Art Center added striking new architecture to the campus. Of the total building cost, local businessman Joseph Lowe and wife Emily provided $150,000. Both were known for supporting young artists eager to study at Syracuse. Emily Lowe, a painter who had exhibited widely, had a show at Syracuse University in 1950.

No ordinary complex, the Lowe Art Center featured terraced outdoor galleries and open-air classrooms. The entire northern exposure, sheeted in prismatic glass, shed evenly diffused light across four classroom studios on the first and second floor. Lowe Art Center also contained exhibition halls, offices of the School of Art, a large lecture room, and a student lounge in the basement, as well as exhibition preparation and storage space.

Tolley scored his greatest coup in arts programming when he hired Yugoslav freedom fighter and sculptor Ivan Meštrović to teach at the Art Center. Syracuse University was on the brink of becoming a major art institution.

Lowe Art Center was designed as a classroom building, yet it could not accommodate all departments of the School of Art. In the summer of 1975 the administrative offices of the College of Visual and Performing Arts were moved to Crouse College. Lowe Art Center was relocated to the former Sims Dining Hall and renamed Lowe Art Gallery. Syracuse University Bookstore took over the former location of the Lowe Art Center. This space was later altered and transformed into the southeast section of Schine Student Center.

As the 1950s ensued, the University could not meet continuing space needs within traditional campus boundaries. Expansion brought new buildings to areas beyond the campus core: Robert Shaw Hall dormitory (1952),

Lowe Art Center (1952), the Women's Building (1953), and the Hoople Special Education Building (1953). Each encroached upon surrounding neighborhoods. Each altered the carefully wrought dynamic between the physical university and its environs.

Then surging postwar enrollment ushered in a period of accelerated student housing construction (1952–62). Dormitories replaced the trailers at Mud Hollow, and classrooms supplanted the Quonset huts. On Mt. Olympus, once a favored toboggan slide, a new cluster of dormitories went up, as outlined by university planner Rotunno. More dormitories were built. Flint Hall (1956) and Day Hall (1958) bore the names of former chancellors. Others dotted the eastern portion of University Hill: Watson Hall (1954), Marion Hall (1954), Dellplain Hall (1961), and Booth Hall (1963). The latter faced Thornden Park where once elegant homes enjoyed commanding views.

In the spring of 1961 the second stage of the building bulge began. Tolley set a goal of $76 million to be raised by 1970, at which time Syracuse University would be celebrating its 100th anniversary.

The University began erecting major academic structures to the north of the Lawn, with I. M. Pei's S. I. Newhouse School of Public Communications the most dramatic addition of this new building era.

42. *Newhouse I, 1964*

Architects: I. M. Pei Associates, New York, N.Y.;
   King & King, Syracuse
Contractor: J. D. Taylor Construction Company

Publishing magnate and SU trustee Samuel I. Newhouse became one of the most generous of donors in Tolley's building bulge. Newhouse gave $15 million to expand the burgeoning School of Journalism, quartered in the Women's Building since 1953. That project evolved into the prestigious S. I. Newhouse School of Public Communications at Syracuse University.

I. M. Pei also designed the Everson Museum of Art in downtown Syracuse.

Newhouse I was intended as first of a three-building complex, each to be connected by a central concrete terrace. Construction began in the spring of 1962 on the site of early dormitory, Haven Hall, which had been torn down along with several cottages.

In designing the building, acclaimed architect I. M. Pei took his cues from Frank Lloyd Wright's unity temple. The building is shaped out of precast concrete in the form of a red cross with three stories under a flat roof. From a height of 32 feet, a multifaceted skylight sheds light on Dedication Hall, which engages the entire center of the building.

Pei called his design an "iceberg" because most of its spaces were underground. Two stories of Newhouse I are submerged under the West Plaza of the "iceberg," totaling almost half of the structure's 76,000 square feet. Within these underground spaces are darkrooms, the Frederic W. Goudy Typographic Laboratory, a two-story photography studio, an advertising sign design studio, two classrooms with combination front and rear projection screens, and a student lounge.

Above ground, the first floor houses the dean's offices, along with a pub-

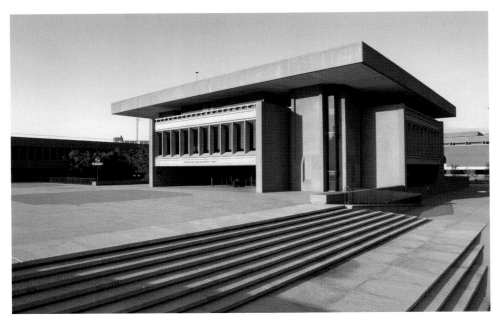

Newhouse I. Courtesy of Syracuse University Archives

lic lounge and a journalism library. The second holds seven large lecture and seminar rooms, an editing laboratory, and news laboratory. The third contains more than twenty offices for journalism faculty members and for seven press associations housed at Syracuse University.

Dedication ceremonies for Newhouse I took place on August 5, 1964. The main speaker was President Lyndon B. Johnson. Crowds were thick and over two hundred reporters were present. The eyes of the world were on SU as President Johnson gave an historic speech divulging deployment of air strikes against North Vietnam in retaliation for purported bombings of American ships in the Gulf of Tonkin.

Newhouse I would become the most applauded example of modern architecture on campus. For his innovative design I. M. Pei received the First Honor Award from the American Institute of Architects.

Many thought that this remarkable surge of campus construction had peaked with the beginning of the Newhouse Center. Yet it would continue for another eleven years.

THE 1960s

Throughout the stormy 1960s, SU became a hotbed of civil rights agitation. Lock-ins, sit-ins, protests, and unrest shook the campus. At the same time urban renewal swept through Syracuse, as it did in other cities throughout the nation.

It is no accident that expansion of SU's physical campus coincided with the heyday of urban renewal. "For SU the urban renewal process with its state and federal funding streams could not have come at a more opportune time." [30]

Two forces were fast at work shaping the campus of the future: the University's own designs for academic growth and the city's plans to revamp University Hill. The consequences of these plans would be considerable and long lasting.

Intending to spread northward as far as Erie Boulevard, the University began to purchase commercial and residential properties. Driven by notions of infinite enrollment growth and a directive to modernize, the University, along with the city and the hospitals, began to remake the face and heart of University Hill. This seemingly endless process peaked in 1966 with the issuance of the University Hill General Neighborhood Renewal Plan, under the aegis of Noreda Rotunno.

Conceived in the modernist spirit of New York State building projects, i.e., Albany's SUNY Campus and Empire State Plaza, the plan proposed an expanded series of quadrangles set into a landscape radically remade for the automobile. It was, in effect, the shape of things to come.

"As the University acquired and demolished structures in surrounding neighborhoods, entire blocks were turned into parking lots. Some buildings, it was expected, would be replaced by new construction. Like many others on campus these were gradually allowed to deteriorate."

In the accelerated rush to build, short-term practicality often preempted long-range planning. Profound departures from the 1966 University Hill

Plan resulted, none more affecting than the construction of Bird Library (1972) on the southernmost block of Walnut Park. Before Bird was built, Walnut Park swept into the Lawn forming a lush greensward between campus core and University Hill. The new library placement was intended to signify the emergence of SU as a major research institution. What it did was effectively to block green access from park to campus, forever altering the relationship between Walnut Park and the Lawn.

43. *Bird Library, 1972*

Cost: $13.8 million
Architects: King & King, Syracuse

Geometrically patterned concrete enriches Bird Library with a sense of strength and texture. While the building makes tactile stylistic references to I. M. Pei's Newhouse design, its scale is more massive, its detail less refined. Renovations of the ground floor were begun in the summer of 2005 to create a "more welcoming, aesthetically pleasing, comfortable environment where members of campus and community can gather to explore and exchange ideas." Current improvements include a café with adjacent soft seating and a repositioning of entrance and exit gates closer to the actual entranceways to open up the entire floor. Future planned upgrades include creation of the

Ernest S. Bird Library. Courtesy of Syracuse University Archives

Joseph Spector Learning Laboratory, a reconfigured services area, several group and individual study areas, and possibly gallery exhibit space.

The William A. Safire Reading Room at Bird Library contains books donated by the noted **New York Times** *columnist, a former SU student and University trustee. It opened in October 1994.*

Named after major donor, Ernest S. Bird (graduate of the Class of 1916, College of Liberal Arts), it is the main library on campus. Over two million volumes can be accessed by some of the most advanced information retrieval technology available.

The 1966 University Hill Plan generated an unprecedented degree of construction and demolition. Steeped in the flawed belief that postwar student growth would be boundless, it would kindle development, even as local and student protest stormed against the adverse side of urban renewal. By the time Bird Library and Newhouse II (1973) were built, this period of aggressive expansion at SU would be over.

THE TWENTY-YEAR PLAN

When Chancellor Melvin A. Eggers was inaugurated in 1971, it was clear that SU had entered a new era. Changing demographics, rising inflation, energy costs, and discontent with higher education brought an end to the notion of limitless enrollment growth.

Unable to build as expected, SU faced yet another dilemma. Construction had soared in years prior, yet upkeep of present buildings had all but come to a halt. How was the school to attract students to a campus with a largely neglected physical plant?

Melvin Eggers conceived a new plan. Maintaining the viability of existing buildings was key. Safety upgrades, energy conservation, structural rehabilitation, and minor improvements showed the way. Extended future life of University infrastructure and past capital investments were the goals. Eggers also focused on completing unfinished buildings left over from the bravado of the Tolley years.

44. *Link Hall, 1970*

Cost: $6 million
Architects: King & King, Syracuse

Ground had first been broken for Link Hall in 1968. Formerly known as Engineering Building No. 2, the building was second in a two-part engineering complex (Building No. 1 was Hinds Hall). Named for scientist and inventor Edwin A. Link, it lines the east side of the Quad and houses many of the classrooms, labs, and offices of the College of Engineering and Computer Science.

Edwin A. Link invented the on-the-ground pilot trainer, which prepared thousands of pilots for air combat in World War II. He also perfected the Apollo Mission and lunar module simulators, which readied astronauts to voyage into outer space.

The structure contains six levels, two underground and four above. With an exterior of red brick and limestone over reinforced concrete, Link Hall replicates a design motif common to newer buildings on the Quad. Its craftsmanship and construction drew special commendation from the Syracuse Society of Architects.

Link Hall

45. *William B. Heroy Geology Laboratory, 1972*

Cost: $2.9 million
Architects: King & King, Syracuse

Specifically designed for the study of geology, Heroy Laboratory took two years to build. It is architecturally unique. Walls are not strictly vertical but angle inward under windows at every floor. Custom bricks adjoin the main vertical with slanted sections. Design choices throughout echo the structure's basic purpose. Expansive first-floor windows are made of bronze glass. Interior colors and materials are geologic in nature with a lobby ceiling of narrow-planked Douglas fir looking down upon slate floors and decorative trees. Note

Heroy Geology Laboratory. Courtesy of Syracuse University Archives

the glass-enclosed staircase from lobby to third-floor reading room, which acts as a greenhouse for the trees.

Heroy Geology Laboratory was named after William B. Heroy, an internationally known petroleum geologist and SU graduate, Class of 1909.

In a display of exceptional functionality, first-floor laboratories contained acid drainage systems that empty chemicals into a neutralizing pit in the basement, and fume systems removed noxious gases used in experiments. On the ground floor one finds a wet tank for waterwave experiments. Other special resources include sample preparation and storage rooms, photo labs, computer clusters, a machine shop, and a 200-seat auditorium.

Rico Lebrun's gripping triptych, *The Crucifixion,* is prominently displayed in the lobby along with two related paintings, *The Cross* and *Ladder of the Cross.* Heroy houses the Department of Earth Sciences.

Even as enrollment kept rising during the late 1960s and into the 1970s, Chancellor Eggers paid close attention to schools and programs that might attract undergraduates.

In spring of 1971 construction was announced for Newhouse II, a second building in the Samuel I. Newhouse School of Public Communications complex (see pp. 97, 127). Made of stark concrete and meant to house the school's broadcast sector, its first two floors held two television studios, a scene shop, and areas for storage. Its third floor contained faculty offices, a 100-seat theater, and a broadcast news laboratory. The dedication of Newhouse II took place in 1975. William S. Paley, then chairman of the board of Columbia Broadcasting System (CBS), was guest speaker. Master of ceremonies was prominent NBC anchor David Brinkley.

During the Eggers era new buildings were erected when demand was apparent or when preservation of existent buildings was not feasible. A perfect example was Archbold Stadium.

Rico Lebrun's The Ladder of the Cross, *Heroy Geology Laboratory*

By 1969, the beloved stadium had fallen into disrepair. The need for a new arena was urgent, but funding efforts were stymied by disagreement over a new site. Several plans for rebuilding were subsequently squelched, and a stadium proposed for the Skytop area ignited local uproar. Electing to build right over the site of the old Archbold, Melvin Eggers undertook the most ambitious project of his administration, construction of the Carrier Dome.

In the winter of 1978–79 Archbold came down. In April 1979 concrete footings for the Dome were poured. Construction proceeded on schedule, despite concerns over environmental issues and minority hiring. On August 29, 1980, the Dome was completed. Along with the Hall of Languages and Crouse College, Carrier Dome would become one of the best-known structures on campus.

46. *Carrier Dome, 1980*

Cost: $26.85 million

Architects: Finch, Heery, Hueber, Atlanta, Ga., and Syracuse

With seating capacity of up to 50,000, Carrier was the fifth-largest domed stadium in the country, the first of its kind in the northeast, the largest to date on a college campus, and possibly the best-known structure at Syracuse University.

More than 80 companies and New York State contributed $27 million to build the Dome (with a $2.75 million major naming gift from the Carrier Corporation)

The Dome was a marvel of size, strength, and engineering ingenuity. Its roof of Teflon-coated fiberglass panels covers an area of six-and-a-half acres. Sixteen fans, each five feet in diameter, inflate and support the 220-ton canopy by creating a difference between interior and exterior air pressure. Fourteen bridge cables, some as long as 700 feet and weighing 7 tons, stitch the roof panels together, sustaining the stadium's immense lighting and sound systems.

Multimillion dollar funding for the Dome was started in part with help from the Carrier Corporation and Melvin C. Holm, then chairman of SU's Board of Trustees.

Since its opening on September 20, 1980, Carrier Dome has brought prominence and national recognition to the University. It is at once home ground to the SU Orange football, men's and women's basketball, and men and women's lacrosse teams. Regional and state scholastic competitions in various sports have been hosted here, as have NBA preseason games. Crowds have flocked to the Dome to see Olympic ice-skating shows and concerts by legendary rock, country, and music stars.

Even as this period saw the creation of the Carrier Dome, a new sensibility emerged that proved to be just as significant: a receptivity to preservation.

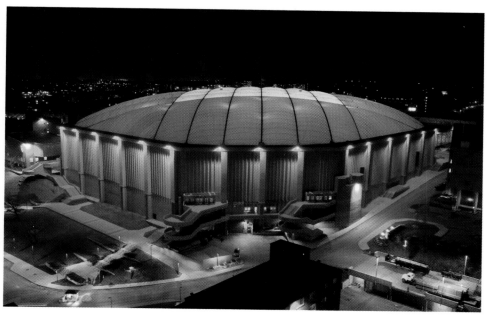

Carrier Dome by night. Courtesy of Syracuse University Archives

Lyman, Smith, Bowne, and Carnegie Halls were all refurbished. Yet the most evident example was in the rehabilitation of the Hall of Languages. That project, small though it was in comparison to the great Dome, signified a dramatic shift in attitude. From now on Syracuse University would consistently view the past as a vital key to planning for the future.

The Carrier Dome ushered in a new building wave, and a strategic plan was forged to address new construction. Virginia Denton in *Syracuse University Campus Plan 2003* explains that "at its core was a clear grasp of the import of balancing two conflicting requirements: a need to enhance and strengthen University academic programs and a need to reconcile capital and current year financial resources."

The Twenty-Year Plan, as it was called, saw new construction as a means of eliminating dependence on inefficient and marginal buildings acquired during the postwar era. New buildings like Crouse-Hinds Hall (1983) and Schine Student Center (1985) rose on campus. Older ones were revitalized. Steele, Smith, and Lyman Halls were renovated, while the Administration Building and Crouse College were restored to lost splendor.

47. *Crouse-Hinds Hall,* 1983

Cost: $5,500,000

Architects: Architectural Resources Cambridge, Cambridge, Mass.; and Sargent, Webster, Crenshaw, and Folley, Syracuse

Designed to meet burgeoning enrollment at the School of Management, this eight-story red brick complex contains ninety-seven offices, twelve class-rooms, several seminar rooms, and a 200-seat auditorium. The Crouse-Hinds Corporation provided a $2.5 million dollar naming gift.

Among other corporate sponsors were the Kresge Foundation, United States Steel Foundation, Booth Ferris Foundation, Rosamond Gifford Charitable Corporation, and Agway, Inc. Enrollment would continue to escalate, and by Spring 2005 a new School of Management would be constructed to provide even more space (see p. 124). Crouse-Hinds Hall now houses the Offices of the Chancellor, Academic Affairs, and Admissions.

Crouse-Hinds Hall. Courtesy of Syracuse University Archives

48. *Schine Student Center, 1985*

Cost: $15 million
Architects: Edward Larabee Barnes Associates, New York, N.Y.

The 1927 Pope-Baum Plan had provisions for a student center that never materialized. Nearly six decades later, Melvin Eggers envisioned such a building as part of a complex involving the Carrier Dome and a hotel.

First came the Sheraton University Inn and Conference Center, dedicated on March 20, 1985. The Schine Student Center followed that spring, thanks to a gift from 1950 SU graduate and trustee Renée Schine Crowne. Crowne named the center after her parents, Hildegarde and J. Meyer Schine. The Schines were founders of an early twentieth-century chain of local/regional cinemas. At one point they owned three movie palaces in downtown Syracuse.

The Schine Center comprises three modern buildings bound by a common court and capped by a pyramid. Within its red brick walls are a cafeteria, lounge, meeting hall, bookstore, and auditorium, and space for student services and community organizations. Although not part of the Historic District, the Schine Center with its rounded exterior arches pays tribute to earlier campus structures in the area. An abstract metal sculpture by Jon Isherwood (1987) adorns the Schine Center Courtyard.

Schine Student Center

49. *Science and Technology Center, 1989*

Cost: $32 million
Architects: Kling Partnership, Philadelphia, Pa.; and Koetter, Kim, and Associates, Boston, Mass.

One of the most crucial academic events of the 1980s was the return to scientific research at SU. University interest in hard research had dwindled over the preceding two decades, largely due to escalating costs and protests over SU/government contracts secured during the Vietnam War. That began to change in the mid-1980s, and in 1986 the University obtained a $27 million loan from the New York State Urban Development Corporation to construct a new Center of Science and Technology.

Casting a postmodern silhouette across five-acres, Sci-Tech was, at the time of its construction, the largest building at SU. Hailed by Chancellor Eggers as a "STATE-OF-THE-ART center . . . to strengthen the area and state economy," the red brick complex was created to improve technological facilities and to create a hub for research and education in computer science, electrical engineering, information studies, and chemistry. The classrooms for each of the departments are located here as well. Also housed in the building is the CASE Center for Computer Applications and Software Engineering.

The School of Information Studies was the first school in the nation to offer a master's degree in information resources management.

Enlightened attitudes helped guide the development of Sci-Tech, namely a renewed respect for the past along with a newfound interest in urban context

Science & Technology Center

and the shaping of open space. Massive as it was, the building effectively shifted the core campus boundary one block to the east. Planned as part of a larger research center, this first phase carefully defined the edge of College Place, establishing open space opposite the east portico of Slocum Hall, a concept originally proposed in the Rotunno plans. Sci-Tech's design took pains to encourage east-west pedestrian movement across its site and into the Main Quadrangle, linking student housing to the east with the core campus.

After CASE Center and Sci-Tech were founded, Melvin Eggers mounted a fundraising campaign that would mark the final phase of his ambitious goals for university expansion.

50. *Flanagan Gymnasium, 1989*

Cost: $5.8 million
Architects: Bolin, Powell, Larkin, and Cywinski, Wilkes-Barre, Pa.

A 115-foot skybridge and lounge links Flanagan Gymnasium to Archbold Gymnasium (1908) and is the newer gym's only means of access. Erected in response to escalating student interest in physical fitness, Flanagan was part of a $1.8 million upgrade to Archbold. Its expanded sports amenities included matted aerobic rooms, volleyball, and racquetball courts. The $5.8 million funding was provided by Lora and Alfred Flanagan, University Funds, and funds to be raised by the Campaign for Syracuse.

Flanagan Gym opened on October 30, 1989, with a widely publicized morning squash match between Chancellor Eggers and Recreation Services Director Nick Wetter.

Flanagan Gymnasium

51. *Dorothea Ilgen Shaffer Art Building, 1990*

Architects: Koetter, Kim and Associates, Boston, Mass.

With its postmodern red brick-and-glass façade, Shaffer is a stylistic cousin to Sci-Tech. Gathered under one roof here were previously scattered University arts programs along with an expanded Joe and Emily Lowe Art Gallery. A signature windowed drum tower firmly anchors the building to the Quad.

Eggers continued to develop the campus through an increased attention to landscaping and to campus art, the latter best exemplified by the corridor sculpture between Shaffer and Bowne.

Shaffer Art Building. Courtesy of Syracuse University Archives

52. *Sculpture Court, 1991*

Three sculptures by Ivan Meštrović (*Moses, Job,* and *Supplicant Persephone*) are on permanent display here along with Louise Kalish's *Saltine Warrior.* Meštrović was a professor of sculpture at SU (1947–55). Two spaces remain open for changing exhibitions by faculty and students.

The University was now clearly building on the legacy of the Revels-Hallenbeck Plan. *The Syracuse University Campus Plan 2003* explains:

> Sims Hall [see p. 38], the former dormitory building from that era, was strengthened by the addition of an imposing new corner entrance. Shaffer Art Building was added to the Sims complex with a main round entrance designed to strengthen the Quad. Likewise the College of Law Library addition further defined the far corner of the West Quadrangle. These projects signaled the beginning of a new allegiance to the original University campus.
>
> At the same time, a seemingly mundane zoning tool called the Planned

Moses, *Sculpture Court. Courtesy of Syracuse University Archives*

Institutional District (PID) emerged as an important factor in shaping the campus. Unlike traditional zoning, which regulates individual land parcels, the PID bundles properties into districts, allowing development requirements to be met over larger areas. For example, traditional zoning may require the provision of a certain number of parking spaces on a specific development site. In contrast, the PID would allow those parking spaces to be provided elsewhere within the site's district.

Syracuse University's PID was developed, in part, to remedy the effects of postwar expansion and increasing public conflict over land use. By encouraging the school to plan its campus as districts, rather than as a collection of individual projects, the PID regulations facilitated planning efforts to build a coherent campus. During the 1980s, PID regulations would become a crucial tool in University efforts to forge a new comprehensive land use plan, one that could build securely upon the legacies of past campus plans and building campaigns.

In 1988 the University undertook the development of a comprehensive land use plan. Focusing on land use and zoning initiatives, the plan established campus boundaries that were formalized as the Area of Interest Land Use Plan.

One of the plan's most visible results was the expanded Maxwell School complex at the heart of the historic core campus. Eggers Hall was developed to triple the size of existing Maxwell Hall, allowing the school to consolidate at one site without giving up its traditional home. The new building reestablished the spatial order initiated by the Pope-Baum Plan. Two new formal campus spaces emerged: a small quadrangle enclosed by the Tolley Administration Building and the academic complex and a second quadrangle centered on the domed Hendricks Chapel.

Eggers Hall crowned a forty-year era of physical expansion that wove a crazy quilt of buildings into an orderly and attractive campus.

"The physical identity of the campus is much better than it was even five years ago," said Bruce Abbey, former dean of the School of Architecture. "There's finally a sense of completeness about the campus that was not there before. The last piece fell into place with the building of Eggers Hall."

At the heart of the 1988 Land Use Plan was an innovative idea: using buildings as tools not only to shape landscape spaces but also to ensure that the quality of the campus improved as it grew larger. A number of concurrent projects illustrated this concept. The 1988 Land Use Plan was based on a simple yet groundbreaking premise: buildings that not only served to shape the landscape but also assured that improved campus quality was synergistic with physical growth. This can be seen in several simultaneous projects, including Eggers Hall and the Center for Science and Technology.

Expansion and upgrading of Day, Watson, and Shaw residence halls, although less dramatic, demonstrated the attractive potential of infill projects and university commitment to on-campus housing. Welcome gains included additional bed space and a considerable reduction in overall density.

The Irving Avenue Garage launched the concept of pairing structured parking with building and landscape projects. Over time, parking had become an essential issue, albeit a politically and aesthetically volatile one. A creative and pleasing solution evolved in the concept of structured parking. A parking garage was too often dismissed as pure infrastructure. The Irving Avenue Garage, however, was developed to enable future building opportunities. While providing critical parking capacity, the garage facilitated the construction of Eggers Hall and the emergence of a formalized West Quadrangle. An open-air bridge overcame obstacles of topography and climate while functioning as a major pedestrian link to the open land of Campus West.

All these projects were completed in association with the 1988 Land Use Plan. All reflected the University's new attitude toward urban design.

The 1988 Land Use Plan was meaningful for the projects it generated; yet its greater significance lay in the ways it defined and directed future growth opportunities. This perception was accomplished with the awareness that a higher level of care is needed to reconcile the University's ambitions with its fixed landholdings and complex urban situation.

Current design criteria and rules for development on such questions as parking, permitted materials, landscaping, and utility infrastructure manage to stimulate rather than hamper admirable architecture.

THE UNIVERSITY SPACE PLAN

I n order to enable both students and school to meet the special demands of today's world, SU has embarked upon a plan for new construction, as well as the expansion and upgrading of older buildings.

Originally known as the Academic Space Plan in 1998, the project was expanded in 2004 to include broader campus needs and retitled the University Space Plan. It is the result of detailed analysis and campus reflection. This plan contains a comprehensive, systematic approach to fulfilling classroom, studio, laboratory, and research needs in a manner that best considers academic, social, and design needs.

As the University looks to the future with its eye on the Academic Plan, it can refer to the University Space Plan to ensure that facilities are optimal. Over the next seven to ten years, SU will add 800,000 square feet of academic and research space at a cost of about $180 million. As described by Patrick Farrell in "A Changing Campus" in *Syracuse Magazine,* these additions include the following:

53. *School of Management Building, 2005*

Cost: $40 million
Architects: Fox & Fowle, New York, N.Y.

In view of an extreme shortage of space, the Martin J. Whitman School was moved from the Crouse-Hinds Building into this new structure in spring 2005. The project offers approximately 160,000 square feet of classroom and office space, or three times the size of the former building, making it the largest single new structure on campus since Eggers Hall (1993). Classrooms offer interactive learning by inspired use of educational technologies.

Whitman School lobby

Every facet of the new building is geared to a quality learning experience—from acoustics and lighting to seating, high-tech teaching stations, and stylish interior design.

Hinds Hall (see p. 95) has been gutted, its interior redesigned for a fresh open place feeling and for collaborative work. Equipped with numerous computer servers and cutting-edge information technology programs, this structure should be the most "wired" building on campus. The new Hinds Hall will contain the School of Information Studies and the Center for Natural Language Processing.

Slocum Hall (see p. 50) will also be thoroughly revamped. The School of Architecture, housed here since 1919, needs new kinds of spaces due to changes in technology. "In the old days, you had a drafting table and a stool," says Virginia Denton, retired director of design and construction at SU. "Today,

Rendering of the new interior, Hinds Hall. Courtesy of Ashley McGraw Architects, PC

computers play a prominent role in architectural design." The College of Visual and Performing Arts shared space with the School of Architecture. Both will relocate downtown (see p. 133) to the former Dunk & Bright Warehouse during the refurbishing of Slocum Hall.

"From an architectural standpoint, the Slocum Hall renovation is one of the more interesting Space Plan initiatives," says academic space planner Christopher Danek. "Plans involve restoring Slocum's skylit, four-story atrium and center hall and may eventually include restoring the 1918 front stairs and grand entry." Renovations will be done in phases with completion expected in 2008. The School of Architecture will move back into Slocum Hall, once renovations are completed. For the first time since its inception in 1873, the School of Architecture will occupy an entire building of its own.

54. *Newhouse III*

Architects: Partnership Polshek, New York, N.Y.

Preliminary plans for the third and final building in the Newhouse Communications Center (see p. 97) were announced in June 2004. The new design will consist of community spaces for faculty and students and a 400-seat auditorium.

At 70,000 square feet, Newhouse III will take over a parking lot and the area next to the Newhouse complex which formerly held satellite dishes. The new building will also strive to create more green spaces around the complex and to maintain pedestrian walkways as seen throughout much of the SU campus. Completion is slated for September 2007.

Under the University Space Plan, other buildings to be extensively renovated for new uses include Crouse-Hinds Hall, Lyman Hall, Slocum Hall, and the Center for Science and Technology.

An 820-car parking structure at University Avenue and Harrison Street, now open for use, is considered essential for new university facilities on the northern edge of the Main Campus.

The University Space Plan is also committed to maintaining the integrity of Walnut Park; several smaller projects involve two properties in that area. Syracuse University campus today is the consequence of over one hundred years of architectural expansion, invention, and often bold policy change. SU today is taking major steps to expand beyond the borders of the Hill, a way of thinking manifest earlier in two satellite campus sites, Greenberg House in Washington D.C., and Lubin House in New York City.

Parking structure, University Avenue

55. *The Paul Greenberg House*

Cost: $2.5 million

Architects: Ripperdaux Architects, Washington, D.C.

Named for SU alumnus (Class of 1965) and trustee Paul Greenberg, this charming four-story house was bought by the University in 1988. Its classic Beaux-Arts exterior of brick and masonry features a two-story portico and etched glass windows installed at the initial renovation. President of his own realty company, Greenberg contributed $1 million toward total purchase and restoration costs.

As a branch campus, Greenberg House strengthens SU's presence in the Washington, D.C., area by encouraging academic, alumni, and recruitment activity through plentiful workshops, seminars, classes, and social events. Its location at 203 Calvert Avenue, corner of Connecticut Avenue, situates Greenberg House in an attractive, vibrant urban area near several embassies. Its programs offer a masters of science in information mangagement as well as government internships and expanded seminars for Maxwell School of Citizenship students.

Greenberg House. Courtesy of Greenberg House

56. *Lubin House*

Cost: $51,000
Architect: John R. Prague, New York, N.Y.

New York City philanthropist Joseph Lubin purchased 11 East 61st Street (1876) as a gift for Syracuse University. Well situated in Manhattan's fashionable Upper East Side, its intent was to "serve the ceremonial and educational presence of Syracuse University in New York City." A first-rate brownstone of the era, its walnut-paneled dining room, art gallery, and library seemed ideal for classes, seminars, and receptions. In 1966 Syracuse bought the house next door, No. 15, a five-story limestone designed by Breen & Nason (1879). Joseph Lubin donated funds in 1981 for its renovation into practical space for the university. SU School of Architecture graduate Richard Hayden (1960) and his firm Swanke, Hayden and Connell redid the interior in 1995. Floors were removed and rebuilt at the same levels as No. 11, and both structures were joined to create new multiuse spaces. Historic interiors were later restored. Originally intended as an alumni center, Lubin House is today the place where metropolitan New York high school students are interviewed for admission. Current students also meet here for special courses, career development, and placement.

Lubin House

DOWN FROM THE HILL
AND OUT INTO THE WORLD

On August 1, 2004, Nancy Cantor became the eleventh (and first woman) chancellor of Syracuse University. In what has been hailed as an "historic move," she announced a dynamic plan for connecting the campus on the Hill to the downtown, forging new and vigorous connections between students at SU and the community at large.[31]

As part of the chancellor's new campaign to "explore the soul of Syracuse," SU is buying or leasing several properties in the downtown area for use by various SU colleges and programs. The game plan, says Cantor, is to place the new schools near "some of the major arts things that are happening. The Museum of Science and Technology, the Redhouse, Delavan, near a lot of the night life and day life of the revitalized Armory Square, and near real neighborhoods where we can really hope to pull in people from the city." [32]

Cantor's vision is steeped in experience-based learning. She points out that students in these programs will benefit from being downtown. Proximity to the businesses and cultural centers related to their studies offers invaluable hands-on educational opportunity.

57. *The Warehouse*

Architects: Gluckman Mayner, New York, N.Y.

Key to the plan is the former Dunk & Bright Warehouse, corner of West Fayette and South West Streets, on the edge of Armory Square. By early January 2006, the School of Architecture had moved into the Warehouse, soon followed by Visual and Performing Arts. Distinguished architect Richard Gluckman, graduate of the SU School of Architecture, was commissioned to redesign the building. Gluckman observed that "the exterior of the building has lost its character, but the bones are extraordinarily good." Not so its skin, he says. Gluckman maintained the strong bones of the building while revitalizing its exterior with parallel rows of windows. Upper floors are tinted shades

The Warehouse

of blue to reduce glare, while golden yellow windows warm the building's body and brighten the downtown landscape.

The Warehouse formerly a blunt, gray box, has been transformed into a vital compliment to school and city. Six floors are slated for initial renovation with ground floor space available for public and community use, including a gallery, 125-seat auditorium, special space for the Cultural Resources Council (CRC) to help local artists benefit from academic resources at the University, a central box office providing easy community access to cultural events within city and University, and retail space.

The School of Architecture will remain in the Warehouse for two to three years while Slocum Hall is renovated. Music and humanities classes will also be held downtown. The sharp industrial-looking structure provides studio space for the Communications Design and Advertising Design Programs and the Goldring Arts Journalism Program. Once the School of Architecture moves back to campus, additional community and university arts programs will make the Warehouse their home.

On the 800 and 900 blocks of East Genesee Street, near Syracuse Stage, a number of leased and purchased properties will be renovated for use by the Drama and Film Departments. These will offer space for specific programs, rehearsal, and performance, including new homes for the Paul Robeson Performing Arts Company and the Community Folk Arts Center.

Once a gracious gateway to the center city, East Genesee Street has recently seen a flurry of revitalization, i.e., such handsomely redone hotels as the Marx, Genesee Grande, and Parkview. It is hoped that a new university presence will spur further development in this vital part of the Hill.

As a result of the SU move more than 550 students are expected to energize the streets of downtown, while learning about and contributing to the well-being of the city center and environs. The University is melding campus vibrance into the existing urban scene, creating a "new city within the old" that "places the University within the center of local and global communities as a resource, contributor, and actively engaged partner."

"What we are doing," observes Mark Robbins, dean of the School of Architecture, "is very standard practice—not only for universities, but also for cities, as they begin to grow and flex. What is unique is the emphasis on the arts as a catalyst." He also points to cultural revivals in the Chelsea, Soho, and Tribeca sections of New York City, which hinged, in part, on the renovation of former warehouse spaces.

One of the most creative proposals in Cantor's plan is a path designed to carry students, residents, and visitors between the Hill and downtown arts and entertainment venues and public spaces.

The Syracuse Connective Corridor, as it is called, will involve a three-mile long twenty-four-hour bus shuttle and pedestrian and bike trails. Lighting and landscape improvements, public art, wayfinding signage, benches, and bus shelters will activate the streetscape with a unique kind of urban artwork and living architecture. In the best tradition of city life, the corridor's walkways promise economic and social rewards related to foot traffic: exploration, interaction, and the vibrant joys of unexpected discovery.

Multiple and symbolic barriers, notably U.S. Interstate 81, seem to render the Hill inaccessible. Intended to dissolve these, the Connective Corridor will present a highly visible insignia of growth and rejuvenation. Beginning near Syracuse Stage on Genesee Street, the path will make its way past the Center of Excellence, envisioned as an intermodal hub for the Corridor.

58. *The Center of Excellence in Environmental and Energy Systems*

Cost: $23 million (approximately)
Architects: Toshiko Mori, New York, N.Y.; with Ashley McGraw, Syracuse

The Center of Excellence is being constructed on the site of the former Smith Corona Typewriter Company just off East Genesee Street. Both private and public funds have been invested in the Syracuse Center, which will be dedicated to creating and exploring innovations in renewable and clean energy sources, especially for "indoor environments." It is fitting that this engineering complex will be built on the site of the former typewriter plant where L. C. Smith made the fortune that enabled him to fund the first engineering school on campus. Smith's factory left a legacy of challenge for architects designing the new Center of Excellence. So contaminated with chromium and asbestos is the original foundation that cleaning or removing it is too costly to be feasible. The new Center of Excellence is being shaped and designed around the perimeters of the older, implacable foundation.

Conceived as a "two-way" route, the Connective Corridor will engage city residents and guests who have previously viewed the campus as off-limits and students who have shied away from the city center. Nancy Cantor speaks of people and ideas traveling up and down the Corridor. "This is a tremendously exciting project," she says. "Syracuse has a well-earned reputation as a crucible for innovative thought. The Connective Corridor will only serve to enhance this by facilitating the convergence of our many talents and energies."

As such, the Connective Corridor holds potential for future development and expansion within the city. Economic impact is expected to spill over into

The Center of Excellence. Designed by Toshiko Mori Architect with Ashley McGraw Architects PC

nearby hotels, museums, entertainment venues, community retail and specialty stores, and restaurants. Not to mention an increase in urban sensitivity and sociological benefit.

Dean Mark Robbins believes the downtown move is particularly appropriate for the architecture school. "Architecture intersects with our daily life at literally every turn," he says. "The earlier students can begin to learn about interacting with people who may be neighbors or clients, the better. Our obligation is to educate students as broadly as possible in a liberal arts tradition, in a history of ideas. When our students graduate and design buildings, those buildings will have more profound links to the city and the community links that are based on an innovative, inventive understanding of the realities of culture and society."

Innovative in conception and scope, the historic move downtown will change SU, in image and substance, from an ivory tower "on the hill" to an embracing global entity. Cantor's plan calls for increased collaboration between SU students and community groups, involvement with neighborhoods such as the South Side, and support for technological and arts projects citywide.

Here is a campus being refashioned for the twenty-first century, one that marries the rich vitality and talent of the University with the cultural wealth and vigorous potential of its host City. Here is a vision that perpetuates that foresight of the school's founders, one that continues to *demonstrate the perfect harmony and indissoluble oneness of all that is valuable of the old and new.*

NOTES

1. "Inauguration of Faculty of Syracuse University," *Syracuse Journal,* July 1, 1904.

2. W. Freeman Galpin, *Syracuse University: The Pioneer Years* (Syracuse: Syracuse University Press, 1952).

3. Ibid.

4. Ibid.

5. Richard G. Case, "SU Highlights: An 1870 Idea Blooms Beautifully," *Syracuse Herald American,* April 26, 1970, p. 40.

6. "Inauguration of Faculty of Syracuse University," *Syracuse Journal,* July 1, 1904.

7. Nottingham and Tucker, *The Highlands* (Syracuse, 1872).

8. Bob Hill, "125 Years in the Life of Syracuse University," *Syracuse University Magazine* 11, no. 3 (spring 1995).

9. David Ramsey, *Syracuse Post-Standard,* Oct. 20, 2002.

10. Ibid.

11. *Syracuse University Campus Plan 2003,* Bohlin Cywinski Jackson Architecture Planning Interior Design Urban Workshop, Syracuse University Office of Design and Construction, Syracuse University, p. 24.

12. *Syracuse Summer Orange,* Aug. 8, 1958.

13. Upton Sinclair, *The Goose-Step: A Study of American Education* (author, 1923).

14. Montgomery Schuyler, "Architecture of American Colleges," *Architectural Record* 30 (July–December 1911): pp. 565–73.

15. *Syracuse Journal,* Oct. 1, 1918.

16. Ibid.

17. Ibid., Dec. 13, 1915.

18. "125 Years in the Life of Syracuse University," *Syracuse University Magazine.*

19. *Syracuse Alumni Magazine,* Fall 1997.

20. *University Herald,* ca. late 1800s.

21. *Syracuse University Campus Plan 2003,* p. 27.

22. *Syracuse Post-Standard,* June 13, 1995.

23. *Syracuse University Campus Plan 2003,* p. 28

24. Ibid.

25. *University Herald,* 1889

26. *Syracuse University Campus Plan 2003,* p. 29.

27. Evamaria Hardin, *Syracuse Landmarks, An AIA Guide to Downtown and Historic Neighborhoods* (Syracuse: Syracuse University Press, 1993), p. 240.

28. Grace Lewis, "S.U. Goes Modern," *Syracuse Post-Standard Pictorial*, December 27, 1953.

29. *Syracuse University Campus Plan 2003*, p. 30.

30. Ibid., p. 31.

31. *Syracuse Post-Standard*, Dec. 12, 1904.

32. Ibid.